DON'T DROWN ON DRY GROUND

ABRAHAM WOODLIFF

Cover Design: Evan Rodda

Cover Photo/Author Photo Credit: Andre Dal Corso

In this short story "Shorelines and Valleys" a partial quote from a poem by Charles Bukowski called "The Genius of the Crowd" is used in conjunction with the Fair Use Doctrine.

 Terran Empire Publishing 1761 Hillside Ct. Placerville, CA USA 95667

www.terranempirepublishing.com

ISBN 978-0-9992022-7-2

DEDICATION

This book is dedicated to a multitude of incredible people who have inspired me and been there for me when I wasn't strong or capable enough to be there for myself.

To my girlfriend - Thank you for brightening my day with your big eyes, dimples and dumb laugh. I love you.

To Jeremy "AnDrEw HURR" Caldwell - You have been my best friend since I was 12 years old, and you believed in me before I even knew what to believe. You will always be my brother. I will never forget the things you did for me when I had nothing.

To Alexandra Bitton - I'm sorry for any and all the pain I caused you. I'm hopeful that one day we can be friends and put the past behind us. Despite everything, I know you're a good person and I truly want the best for you.

To the Bitton Family - I know things are difficult since Alex and I split, but I will always love you. I never really had a family and your family made me realize life was possible.

To Tèa Svorcan - You were always supportive of my writing and I'll never forget your kind words and the bookmark you gave me. I'm proud of all that you have accomplished, Yung Shark.

To Sam Melton - Even though we don't talk, you had a profound impact on me. I'm not going to explain because you know.

To Ricky Rat - Even though we're from different circumstances, you never made me feel less than and you've always been a tremendous friend... Also, your mom is really nice.

To Stuart "BROKE ASS STUART" Schuffman - Thanks for giving me a platform for my writing. I've always admired your open mindedness and ability to survive as a writer in San Francisco. You're dope, Stu'.

To the San Francisco Chronicle/SFGATE - As a kid who grew up in the Bay Area, you will never know what it meant to me when you asked me to pitch an article. I didn't even know you guys paid attention to me as a writer and when I'm depressed, I look back on that and remember not to give up.

To The Bold Italic - Thanks for giving me a shot!

To Robert and Terran Empire Publishing - I know it took a while, but we fucking got it done! Thanks for giving me this shot and believing in me as a writer.

To my mother and father - Thanks for giving me a lot to write about, I guess.

To my brother Isaac - I know Heaven probably doesn't exist, but if it does, I hope that you're proud of me. You know better than anyone how unfair life can be since yours was snatched from you while still in infancy. Though the time we spent together was short, I'll never forget you and you'll always be my baby brother. I carry you with me everywhere. I wish I didn't because it hurts, but in some capacity, it means you're alive as long as I am, and that gives me comfort. You inspired the name of this book. Despite the trauma of finding you dead which made me understand that our family had problems that were different from most of the kids I grew up around, I'm still trying to find happiness. I hope you do too. I'm sorry I couldn't save you.

To the 200k followers of Bay Area Memes - Thanks for following. Even if you hate on me, I am thankful that you even care enough to do that.

To anyone I forgot - Sorry I suck.

INTRODUCTION

The fact that I'm even writing an introduction for a book, let alone my book, is a surreal experience. To be completely transparent with you, I never honestly thought that this day would come. I dreamt about it, envisioned it, and it always felt far away. It felt impossible. But, as life has proven so many times before, nothing is impossible, but a lot of things are unlikely, and this certainly felt unlikely. For most of my life, I've struggled with an inability to open up. I've masked my emotions behind humor and a feigned display of aloofness. The thought of displaying care, vulnerability, or really anything that couldn't be categorized as a joke made me anxious. To this day, it fills me with intense anxiety that I'm trying to work through. However, all rules have their exceptions. Writing has been my exception. Emotions that I found to be too complex or awkward to articulate fell flatly onto the page. Angst, sadness, longing, loneliness, and love became easy to express, as long as it was written rather than said.

When I was 16 years old, I attended a continuation school called Vicente Martinez High School in Martinez, California, a small refinery town that sits on the East Bay's outskirts. It was there that I discovered a poem entitled "Bluebird" by a writer named Charles Bukowski. It shook me to my core. I never realized poetry's importance until that day.

I never realized that so much beauty and relatability could be conveyed so effectively in so few words. After that, I started writing. Most of it was stupid and formless. My writing was too raw, overly emotional, and bitter. I destroyed most, if not all of it.

As time went on, I kept writing secretly. I was able to focus and say what I wanted to say. Things I otherwise lacked the courage to speak. I didn't fill the page with unnecessary words to prove my intellect to any nil audience anymore. The more I wrote, the better I felt. No matter what was going on in my life, the writing was like a secret window that provided a bit of sunlight only meant for me to see. It was the only thing that felt right in a life that seemed so wrong. I became more ambitious with my writing. I began working on short stories, novels (all of which remain unfinished) and decided to give articles a try. After initial failure, I finally caught a break with a San Francisco-based webzine called *The Bold Italic*. It was the first time I had been paid to write, and even though the pay wasn't much, the fact that someone felt my writing was worth anything filled my heart with joy. Most of the articles I wrote were borderline garbage. Nonetheless, I was happy to keep their dumpsters full of my hacky excrement.

After some time writing for *The Bold Italic*, I began running into issues. Particular articles that were initially greenlit were rejected for reasons that I won't get into here. Still, it frustrated me, and I decided if I wanted to write, I needed to control what comes out. So, like every other great writer before me... I created a meme page. And to my surprise, the page became successful.

Despite the page's success and the opportunities, it presented, I still felt bogged down by a lingering depression. No amount of good that came into my life seemed to alleviate its burden, and that is precisely what inspired the title of the book you're holding in your hand right now. Life is unpredictable, and bad things happen to the best and worst among us. Because of this unpredictability and the scars left by misfortune, we live lives of inhibition and fear. We guard ourselves against others. We stop creating, socializing and we end up dead long before our bodies have the good sense to die. We don't see the possibility of the present because our minds are hardwired to reflect on the pains of the past, robbing us of the oxygen needed to move forward, thus contaminating the future. We die before we get there.

So, remember...

Don't Drown on Dry Ground.

-Abraham Woodliff

FOREVER IN BLUE JEANS

I consider my relationship with my father unorthodox at best. It could be characterized as horrible at worst, but that doesn't change the fact that moments that still linger and make me wonder what he could have been, had the dealer who dealt him his cards in the casino called life been less cruel.

My father wasn't a free man. He was shackled by something. A tangible trauma. I don't know the origin of this trauma; he never spoke of it, but it could be felt, and if you stared into his dark brown eyes, it could be seen hiding behind his pupils, coloring his view of the world.

After sundown on select weekends, my father found a diamond and told the whole neighborhood about his discovery. My parents' bedroom had windows that overlooked Patterson Avenue, just a few hundred feet from where it intersected with MacArthur Boulevard. He had a JVC stereo system: 5-disc-changer, dual tape deck, two speakers with a subwoofer that was optional but allowed for a more bass-rich listening experience. On these special nights, my father would place two ice cubes in his snifter and pour himself a glass of scotch; then, he'd pour himself a few more. After downing his third or fourth round, the stereo was on, and the sound of Neil Diamond's music, completely in sync with my dad's voice, echoed off of East Oakland's scarred concrete.

The beginning of my father's performance always started with something triumphant. "We're coming to America today," he'd sing as he raised his glass out of our window into the cool bay air. I used to come out of my bedroom to watch him. I stared in awe as his body would move wildly to the rhythm of the instruments, and his face would match the emotions suggested by the inflection of Neil's voice.

All of our neighbors got a front-row seat to my father's show, but I was one of the lucky few who was blessed with a backstage pass. Not everyone in the audience was a fan. His renditions of Neil's greatest hits also attracted their fair share of hecklers. Sometimes the neighborhood hustlers who sat on stoops or gathered in front of liquor stores would loudly laugh at my dad, or they'd scream "shut the fuck up," but my father didn't listen. He wouldn't lower his voice or turn off the music. He just continued to pour his soul out into the void and his scotch into the glass.

By the middle of his set, the songs my father chose to sing were less about triumph and more about belonging. These were songs about finding a place to call home and coming to terms with the fact that life on this big blue ball, floating through an ever-expanding nothingness, seems to have everything except an instruction manual. Deep down, we know there's no right or wrong way to go. The world's leaders are just passing down tradition, and the laws aren't rooted in logic but conservation of the known. No matter what system or nation it governs, each piece of legislation is inked with the blood of those deemed too critical to exist within it. There's nothing special in these institutions, and with this realization, there's nothing left to do but live. Neil Diamond knew it, and I know my father knew it. I could tell from the passion that exploded from his chest as he sang.

"I am!' I said to no one there, and no one heard at all, not even the chair... 'I am!' I cried. 'I am!' said I, and I am lost, and I can't... even say why!" He may not have been able to express it in his own words, but he knew.

My father's drunken singing was a part of my life for years. Each performance came with a different setlist, but one song was always included: "Forever in Blue Jeans." The song was released in 1978 on Neil Diamond's double-platinum record; You Don't Bring Me Flowers.

When I started this story, I said my father wasn't a free man, and that remained true throughout his life, but when he sang this song, he was free. He looked like freedom. He moved like it, sang like it, lived like it. The shackles that restricted him were gone. He was weightless. There was a grace to his movements that I haven't witnessed in anyone else.

My father was diagnosed with cancer earlier this year. He will likely be dead before 2020 ends. My father's impending death made me realize that he wasn't actually alive for much of his life. His heart was beating, but he didn't always have a pulse. Despite this, I refuse to remember him as a lifeless man. Instead, I will remember lessons he taught me with the songs he sang to me and anyone who would listen on Patterson Avenue. He taught that while money talks, it doesn't sing or dance, and it doesn't walk, and as long as those lessons are here with me, his memory will be...

Forever in Blue Jeans, Babe

The Laurel

I sat in the Laurel looking for you

Waiting to feel the nostalgia of youth's embrace

But inspiration comes when it wants

The chipped paint of the blue house on Patterson Avenue did little for me.

When I was little, it did a lot.

My father and I sat in that house.

Near the corner of Patterson and MacArthur

He'd sing Neil Diamond to an adoring audience of absolutely no one.

But he sang anyway.

He sipped scotch while I played Sega Dreamcast

And I didn't know anything about life.

And that was the greatest gift anyone could ever offer.

Ignorance.

It's not bliss.

It's just the belief that there can be.

Don't read too much.

Leave Google alone.

Don't look for answers.

Because you may find them.

And when you do, the hope dies.

And there's nothing left to replace it with.

Value of a Memory

Chipped paint

Rusted

Chain link

Fence
It stands there.
Its foundation strong
The furniture is covered in plastic
There were people here once.
In that house
They lived in there.
In that house.
Their urine still stains the toilet bowl.
Their hair follicles are still intertwined into the carpet
The walls still faintly smell of grandma's perfume
The stove is still slick with splotches of grease.
From bacon.
Cooked.
By people
Who
LIVED
In that house.
Now they're alive
But they don't live there
Anymore.
The lord
Of
The land
Said
No.
Your hair isn't worthy of the carpet.
Your bacon doesn't taste good enough.
Your grandma's perfume isn't sweet enough

You have to go.

Leave your life behind.

You can't live

Here

Know your worth

And today someone decided

It's worth more than you here.

Magicians

When I reminisce on happiness

My mind wanders down Patterson Avenue

Until it reaches the blue house that hugged the corner of MacArthur

I remember the Transbay bus and the bright lights of San Francisco reflecting off the thick plastic

windows marred by scratches and filth.

We'd get picked up at the terminal and taken to my aunt's apartment across the street from El

Faro in the Mission

I remember begging them to take me to Chinatown

Just to watch the red lanterns blow in the fog rich wind of the Pacific

I remember rides through the Caldecott to my grandma's trailer in Concord.

The overcast of the shoreline was rapidly replaced by the sun of the Diablo Valley.

And the mountain's multiple peaks blessed my eyes

Childhood has the ability to make the mundane feel like magic

And if you spend your childhood in a magical place
The magic is magnified
But then we grow up
And the magic seems to fade
So, we spend the remainder of our lives
Searching for the magicians
We once were.

Albany Hill

You're sitting in your car.
You're parked at the top of a long winding slope
Albany Hill:
A lump of greenery surrounded by bustle
Surrounded by us.
You look to the west:
San Francisco
You look to the east:
Humanity on the hillsides
Quarantined
You look straight ahead:
You see a young Jewish father
Yarmulke clipped to his uncharacteristically straight
Hair
He has two young children by his side
Both boys.
His children look similar to you at that age.
They're fussy.
They don't understand.

That they're free.

For now.

DISHWASHER

Sushi King is the name of the Japanese restaurant I work at in San Francisco's Japantown. It's a tourism hub for anime enthusiasts masquerading as its own neighborhood. Once upon a time, Japanese immigrants inhabited this neighborhood on their entry into America with hopes of a better life. The real estate costs of Japantown assure that that is no longer a possibility for anyone, Japanese or not. Japantown is surrounded by The Fillmore District, a once Black enclave that is now home to neglected public housing and murals to influential former residents. Gentrification brought millionaires and the businesses that cater to millionaires so that sometimes you almost forget housing projects surround you. San Francisco, in a nutshell.

My name is Tony Wu. I'm Chinese. I don't live in Chinatown. I live in Ingleside. It's a place where real San Franciscans live and tourists never venture into, so naturally, you've never heard of it. The rest of the Sushi King's staff are also Chinese, except for the chefs; they're Japanese, a minority in Japantown. Some customers try speaking Japanese to our staff, despite many of them being from China. It didn't matter. This is America. Nuance is scary. Enjoy the ramen, the anime-themed ambiance, and the lie that this is what Japan is like. I've never been to Japan, but I assume six city blocks of ramen stands, sushi places, Attack On Titan, and Hello Kitty merchandise doesn't offer the full experience. Suppose we could incorporate the 100-hour-work-week, staggeringly high suicide rates, fingerless gangsters, or the enforcement of extreme conformity by way of social exclusion into the tourism experience. Then maybe I wouldn't be so jaded at the adoration for a land of a rising sun they've never seen.

I'm a dishwasher. I wash dishes. That's why I'm called a dishwasher. In a world filled with ambiguous titles meant to obscure the fact that you're not genuinely essential to a company's operation, my title offered no such ambiguity. I washed dishes, so they called me a dishwasher. I shared the same title as machines that did the same thing as me. There was no doubt in my employer's ability to replace me.

"Tony, we need you at the register," Patrick said. Patrick was my boss. His father owned Sushi King. We never really saw his dad, the Sushi King, very often. He was probably too busy counting cash atop his sushi-throne in his sushi-castle and fucking his sushi-wife in her big, fat sushi-ass. Patrick had this annoying habit of assigning people to the register at will. I hated working the register. It's not that I disliked people; it's just when people transform into customers, they're no longer people, they're customers, and trust me, there's a huge fucking difference between a person and a customer.

"Okay, give me a second. I gotta dry my hands."

"Quickly," Patrick replied with a tone that poorly hid his impatience.

There was a massive line. Every weekend it seemed that there was some kind of event that took place in Japantown. Unfortunately, this particular week was one of the biggest of Japantown's annual events: The Anime Expo.

Demographically speaking, it's a sociological anomaly. You have traditionally beautiful women dressed up as cartoon characters and men who are either pencil-thin or excessively obese with all the grace and social ability of a bull in a china shop. And the bull just so happened to be on the autism spectrum.

Smooth criminals.

The first guy I rang up was the smoothest.

"Your palms must sweat a lot," he said as he anxiously stared over at the girl beside him with anticipation of some validation. She didn't give a verbal response. Only a placating nod. It was not a signal of an agreement or disagreement, just an acknowledgement of the noise coming from his throat.

I stared at him for a moment. I wasn't offended. His alpha-male inspired effort, well, his alpha-male effort within the context of being in line at a sushi restaurant while poorly cosplaying had backfired. I gave him his total.

"That comes to $38.54. Are you paying with cash or credit?"

He dug out a crumpled assortment of cash from his pocket: a twenty, three fives, seven ones. Before I could even verify that he had given me enough to cover the bill, he grabbed his tray of food, spilled soup on his sushi, blurted "keep the change," and quickly walked away. I kept the change.

Smooth criminal.

My fingers were pruney from the dish pit. Which, I admit, despite it being entirely normal, is a peculiar sight when exchanging money with a stranger. I'm 31, and my hands are age-appropriate. However, after bussing tables and washing dishes for a few hours, my body remained suspended from the standard time continuum. Still, my hands are taken on an accelerated journey through time to movie theater discounts, xenophobia, and erectile dysfunction by way of nature's most fantastic resource and hand-specific time machine: H_2O.

I was apathetic as I rang up customers. The faces blended into one excessively hungry, undefined mess of humanity. Ramen and Sushi. That's all anyone really bought. That's all anyone really knew. My elderly-looking hands became more efficient at swiping cards, stuffing cash, and passing plates as my mind left, and I became the ideal worker: a body without a soul.

And then I saw her. My soul returned, and my efficiency decreased with complete disregard for the faceless, fascist universal dictator we lovingly refer to as Money.

To say I found her beautiful would be an understatement. Her eyes held the vastness and mystery of the ocean. Her hair perfectly framed her face. Her lips suggested a legitimate case for intelligent design as they seemed to have been created to emphasize seduction.

I remember thinking to myself, 'how dare you come here and ruin my life with your presence.'

She just stood at the register.

I didn't want to stare directly into her eyes. They seemed to possess a capability to gaze beyond your physical body and observe your essence. The prolonged silence only exacerbated my anxiety.

"What can I do for you?" I asked in a dismissive tone so cavalier that it seemed suspicious. Nothing says you care more than tones expressed purposefully to accentuate your lack of it.

She stared at me. Stared through me. Her eyes rendered me transparent.

"Listen, if you're not going to order something or if you're unsure of what you want, please move so other customers can make their orders," I said.

She parted her lips and looked at me with a confused expression.

"What are you even doing here?" She asked.

"What does that mean?"

"You know what that means. What are you even doing here?"

"I'm... working."

"What does that mean?"

"It means I'm working. Are you okay?"

She smiled and coyly replied, "Are you?"

I paused. I didn't know who this woman was. She was beautiful and clearly insane. It almost felt like she was trying to flirt with me. I just stared at her. My heart rate elevated.

She grabbed me by my collar and pulled me toward her with a strength that her small frame concealed. She pressed her lips against mine. I went with it. It felt like it was meant to happen. She bit my lip as I pulled away from the kiss.

"Who are you?" I asked.

She stared into my eyes with the intensity of an earthquake and said, "Let's go."

Although I knew it was reckless, we did go. I just walked from the register and through the crowd of hungry patrons who were as confused as I was. I didn't know why I followed this woman. I just did. I followed my heart through the judgmental eyes of the crowd. Patrick rushed out of the backroom and shouted, "Tony, what the hell?" I didn't give him an answer to that question because the Hell was obvious. This was the Hell. I wasn't trying to escape to Heaven. I just didn't want to be in Hell anymore. She tightly gripped my hand as we walked out of Sushi King together.

Not every revolution needs to begin or end with a beheading. Sometimes just acknowledging that the king is just as human as you, but on the right side of pretense, is more of a punishment than anything else could be.

Hand in hand, together, we escaped the crowded central plaza of Japantown and strolled down Post Street. We talked and laughed. Our movements were in unison as if one soul had inhabited two bodies. I wondered if this was what true love was. A popular theme in media is the idea of 'love at first sight.' Was this what had occurred?

"Are you from 'The City?'" I asked.

"I'm from you."

I took that as a sign that she wasn't from 'The City.' People who are really from 'Frisco' rep it. No ambiguity. People who pass through 'The City' in their attempt to cultivate an identity or the masses in search of tech wealth are the ones who gave vague answers. It didn't matter. Her smile was hypnotic. I looked into her eyes and felt I had known her my entire life. Our bodies may have never met, but our souls had been on speaking terms long before the encounter at Sushi King. This reality was the only truth that mattered.

We made it to the intersection of Post and Fillmore. Since I knew she probably wasn't from here, I had an idea.

"Wanna see something famous?"

"What, like the Golden Gate Bridge?"

"Nah, that's too famous, too far, and there's always too much traffic. Have you seen the 'Painted Ladies' before?"

"Even if I have, it'd feel like the first time if it was with you."

So that's where I decided to take her.

We strolled down Fillmore. The money needed for a degree in sociology seemed superfluous to me. Why attend college and waste years of your life in an attempt to learn about the contrasts of society in a classroom when you can witness it all for free in the Fillmore District?

We passed yuppies, millionaires, and homes worth more than the annual GDP of developing nations. We strolled past hustlers that congregated around corner stores as they sold anything they could sell under the watchful eye of Jazz musicians immortalized in murals celebrating the area's former status as the 'Harlem of the West.'

I felt well-informed and important as I pointed all the significant spots on Fillmore Street to her. I pointed to a food vendor that was known for selling greasy onion rings.

"That was mentioned in an Andre Nickatina song."

She looked up at me and smiled. I took it as a sign that she didn't know who that was, but then she surprised me.

"I smoke chewy like a mutha' fuckin' nut!"

"Oh my God, you do know!" And almost as if I was obligated, I finished the line.

"You gotta gram bag hit the zags and roll her up," I said giddily.

"Cuz a..."

She paused. We both knew why she paused. We both laughed. And then we were quiet. The silence wasn't one that signified an awkward pause. It was a contented silence. The type of silence that was a pleasure to share. It was the type of silence only a few could genuinely understand because only a few have ever experienced it. It was the satisfactory silence of knowing that words were no longer needed. The connection was solidified, and all that was left to do was bask in the esoteric wisdom that soulmates exist. No conversation required. We both just knew.

In what seemed like an instant, we made it to Alamo Square: the park where tourists would congregate to either begin or end their time in San Francisco with a bit of Full House nostalgia. I let go of her hand and pointed to the 'Painted Ladies.'

"There they are."

"Touristy or not, they're beautiful," she said.

"I know. But that's the problem, everyone knows. Everyone knows about everything now. Nothing seems special in San Francisco anymore."

"You're special."

My heart fluttered, and I kissed her. The kiss wasn't sexual. The kiss was thankful. Thankful for freedom. Thankful for her. Thankful that in a city of a million faces and a billion ideas, I stood out.

Neil Armstrong needed science and a rocket to leave the planet. All I needed was her.

We walked along Steiner Street to the stairs that led into the center of Alamo Square. We made it to the top and stopped for a moment. The play structure that greeted us rarely hosted playful children, just adults who day drank and did anything they could to live a lifestyle reminiscent of the advertisement that brought them to San Francisco in the first place.

None of them seemed unique. They looked like extras in the same bland romantic comedies that come out every year

You know the ones where a high-powered career woman and a man, usually in some kind of creative pursuit, fall in love after they meet in line at a chic bakery where the ruggedly handsome, yet tragically poor man has a rough exterior but a soft interior?

Eventually, they have passionate sex in the wealthy woman's loft (always a loft) with exposed brick and skyline views of <insert prominent American, possibly European city (accent optional) here.>

But then they have a petty fight. Presumably, a class-related conflict where the man felt uncomfortable after attending some party with rich people and got embarrassed after telling her rich friends that he worked as a janitor and did street art on the side. After the break-up, they bump into each other at a farmers' market where poor people never are in the first place. Still, somehow, he was there because, in the perfect world of cinematic fantasy, the poor can afford fresh produce, and they fall back in love.

These people all looked like they saw these movies and decided to take their bottomless bank accounts out of their boring Midwestern hometowns for a coding job and a starring role in the big city that won't ever come.

But then again, who was I to criticize them? My hatred wasn't for them but for the fact that our coexistence seemed impossible. Not because of anything they individually did, but because their presence equated to my removal. I cleaned their dishes, and they changed the world. I'm not factored into the change they envisioned, but none of that mattered at the moment. I was free.

I led the way to a bench with a direct view of the 'Painted Ladies.' We sat together. San Francisco was still beautiful. It was just too hard to appreciate its striking beauty before. It is hard to enjoy anything when you're hunched over a sink with moist, wrinkled hands eight hours a day. A dish pit is a dish pit, whether you're in San Francisco or Alabama.

"I know we're in one of the most beautiful places in the world, but it's nowhere near as beautiful as you are to me."

I reached for her hand, but there was nothing there. I looked over and reached again, but nothing.

I was on the bench by myself.

I couldn't have been on the bench alone. I had to know if this was some kind of joke that she had played on me.

I approached a man drinking from a bottle of expensive-looking wine, partially covered in a brown paper bag. We had passed by him on our way to the bench.

"Excuse me, you saw me walk to the bench with a girl, right?"

"Uhh, no. You just walked up alone with a smile on your face. Seemed like you smoked a bag of some good tree. By the way, if you need any more, I got you, bro. No shady shit either. All legit shit. My boy, Broderick, has a weed delivery start-up called Buzzdoor... Because we bring the buzz to your door. Get it? Ha!"

"I'm good, man, but you're sure I was alone?"

"Yeah, you were alone. Anyway, bro, to download the Buzzdoor app, all you gotta do is go to..."

"I'm good. I don't smoke."

"Well, if weed isn't your shit and you need some blow, there's no app... Yet! Ha! But I know a guy in The Castro, gay as fuck, but his coke is pure Colombiano, my dude. But you look like you might be a 'China White' kinda guy. Haha! I'm kidding, bro. I'm actually really PC, but this wine brings the 'sav' roasts out of me."

I turned around and walked toward the stairs. She wasn't fucking real.

She wasn't fucking real.

I was on the bench alone.

I am still alone.

I looked around one more time to make sure, and there was no sign of the woman who saw me and freed me. The only familiar ladies that stood before me were the painted ones and the day drinkers, as they waited on their co-stars who seemed to run perpetually late.

A tear escaped my left eye and streamed down my cheek as I descended the steps back to Steiner Street. My head hung down. I crossed Steiner onto Grove until I reached Fillmore.

I passed the hustlers, the yuppies, the onion rings, and the immortal Jazz musicians

I passed the cafes, the corner stores, the wine bars, the concert venues, and the projects, but I knew I was alone this time. And nothing is worse than knowing you're alone.

As I made it back to the intersection of Post and Fillmore, I held my hand out. There was a part of me that expected her to grab it. I wanted to feel the warmth of her hand interlocked with mine again, but she didn't hold it because she never did. She wasn't there. She never was, yet I had some sort of sentimental attachment to that specific spot.

The spot where I had fooled myself into thinking she was there. I didn't want to leave it, for there was still an ounce of hope in my heart that she or the insanity that manifested her would return.

A hopeful ache.

I snapped out of my daze and thought about my job. I wondered if I still had a job. Patrick would have had every right to fire me. The quickest way to be kicked out of the sushi kingdom is by crossing one of the crown's heirs, and my recent hallucination probably qualified as such an offense.

My stomach dropped as I approached the Japantown Plaza. Despite all that had happened or didn't happen with me, everything looked as it had when I left. Anime nerds from all four corners of Northern California had swarmed Japantown in their best and worst costumes. Food vendors and cheap anime merchandise peddlers were all over the place, and everyone seemed content, if not satisfied, in their fandom or profits made as a result of someone else's.

I took a deep breath as I approached Sushi King.

Before I went inside, I looked around, and I hoped to see her, but she wasn't there. So I walked into the restaurant that I had thought just an hour prior I had permanently rid myself of.

It was even more crowded than before. Christina, Patrick's 15-year-old daughter, was ringing people up in my absence. She looked stressed. Her father was too hard on her and would make her fill in when employees called out sick. Just the same as the Sushi King himself had done to Patrick when he was a teenager. It appeared that Patrick would make a fine Sushi King when his father eventually choked to death on a caviar-coated California roll. Patrick and I made eye contact.

"Tony, can you come into the back so we can speak for a moment?"

I was about to get yelled at. I've been yelled at before, though. So I knew what to expect from the interaction that awaited me.

"Tony, what the fuck? Do you even want this job?"

I didn't respond, but I assumed he meant that as a rhetorical question, considering I had just manifested a love interest out of thin air and abruptly left mid-transaction. Still, due to economic considerations and potential mental health inquiries, I kept my mouth shut.

"You just stared at a customer, starting laughing, and walked off! What is wrong with you? If you didn't want to ring people up, you could've just said so."

Bullshit.

"So, do you want this job or what?"

"I do," I said.

"Then fucking act like it! What even happened back there?"

"I had a panic attack and didn't know what else to do except laugh, I guess? I've struggled with anxiety and depression for most of my life, and I was overwhelmed by the crowd."

"That's great, and all, Tony, but you're an adult, and when you're an adult, you gotta swallow shit. Do you think I'm not anxious? My father and I deal with the city passing laws making it hard to run a fuckin' lemonade stand, let alone a full restaurant. And now I'm forced to pay $16.50 minimum to employees who just decide to have panic attacks and leave whenever they please."

"I'm sorry, Patrick."

"Well then, show me you're sorry by washing these dishes. They've been piling up while you were contemplating whether you felt like working or not."

"Thank you."

"Don't thank me. If you ever pull some shit like that again, you're fired," Patrick said as he stormed out of the kitchen into the dining area.

I walked to the sink and put on my apron. At that moment, it felt like the heaviest thing in the world. I felt like I had just placed a boulder on my back, and now I'd be forced to carry it for as long as I physically could.

I picked up the first plate. I scraped the uneaten food off, turned on the faucet, and watched the water go down the drain...

The Point

I don't really know what I'm doing

But I know what I'm not doing

And in some ways

That can be more valuable.

I'm not writing for wine moms

Nor am I writing for white geriatric women that brag about banging jazz musicians

You know, before they settled down with your compromise of a father.

I write for the perpetual procrastinators

The ones that sit at bus stops

On their way to a job you probably look down on

Lost in their daydreams

Fantasizing about what their lives could be if they had the energy and the courage

To live one.

The people with the projects unfinished

The chores undone

The ones whose depressed days lead to misspent decades

I write for the aching backs in Richmond's warehouses

And the suicidal ideation common among cubicle dwellers in Walnut Creek's entry level office jobs.

The ones where you have to dress like you make 6 figures for someone to pay you 5.

Where the posters show people smiling with dead eyes, stiff hair and white teeth.

In the hell where handshakes are meaningless and pleasant-ries are endlessly pursued despite being pointless.

I write for the pointless.

And that's the point...
I guess.

Chasing Your High

Like an addict
I chase your high
Rich with expectation
Poor in experience
I pour myself out into an ocean of you
Hoping to float
Expecting to drown.
My charisma is caffeine
My anxiety is withdrawal
So I become withdrawn
Accompanied only by intrusive thoughts
Fears eating other fears
Inspiring violence
Which sits inside of me
Withering away
Eating at the lining of my stomach
Filling my heart with something other than blood
But at least I have something to write about.
But I often wonder
If it's worth reading.

Burn Alive

America
HATES
The underdog

But

Loves

The underdog story

Everyone wants to tell their underdog story

They watch movies

And montages

With fast music

They watch men climb hills

Women push out babies

Firefighters kick in doors

To buildings

Set *ablaze*

But these people

Have never

Been set

On

Fire

And would

Burn

Alive

If

They were

No Giant

I'm going to San Francisco

Where all the things that have an effect on my life happen

Where my father ended up.

Where my mother was born

Where the ground shakes and the Giants live.

But I'm no Giant,

I just look like one.

North Beach

The poets in San Francisco during the '50s and '60s sat around North Beach

Twiddling their thumbs in cafes

Hunched over typewriters in studio apartments

Writing a lot of trash and mining a bit of gold

The 49ers of the beat era

True team players

Small rooms, cheap drinks and emotional men before the internet told you that that was okay in a self-empowerment post written by someone who wants to be empowered by a collection of likes from people that no one loves

They protested wars.

No country for old men

But no property for the young ones

We don't congregate in North Beach's cafes as they've upped their prices to the point of alienation

And the screams of the unhoused and unhinged distract from the words that want to flow out of open wounds like vertical cuts over healthy veins or clouds that produce torrential rains over ever-moving oceans that rise with overabundance as the land it rightfully reclaims simultaneously dies of thirst

The rising tide won't lift all boats

That was a lie.

It will only provide proof

That some vessels

Were meant to sink.

God bless San Francisco

The city of the Golden Gate

Stained yellow with piss

Because gold has become the gatekeeper

I'm Not Sure

I don't know if it's possible for me to be like them.

No amount of envy can motivate the mountains that would need to be moved in order for me to achieve a connection with the tattered cord connected to my heart.

I just want to feel normal.

I want to speak without anxiety.

I wonder how they make it seem so effortless.

Have you seen people in love?

Have you felt the energy of a room shift when the electricity between two beings is circulating?

Circulating past you.

Through you,

But never in you.

You smile.

They smile

They talk to you

You talk to them

You make mental notes.

More analysis added to the archives

For the research that never ends

Quick witted quips escape from my mouth every now and then

But the right person never seems to hear them.

I just replay the words in my head.

Preparing for the recital
I'm never able to attend.

Raise the Dead

Take the corpses of the people that were murdered in impoverished cities

Dump the caskets at the doorsteps of their employers

If they had an employer

If they were a child take them to where their parents work.

Let the blood soak the paperwork at the supervisor's desk.

Let the stench of decay fill the offices of the pencil pushers

whose purpose is nothing more than figure out ways to get more out of people for less

Bury them alive in the coffins shared with the deceased.

Leave them there with their thoughts under six feet of dirt for 24 hours.

Dig them up.

Ask them for a raise.

DESTINY

The lights flickered above her head as she attempted to adjust her eyeliner in preparation for the next client. The cracked mirror only further obscured her view. She glanced at her phone and saw she had less than 30 minutes before her next scheduled appointment began. Without thinking, she grabbed her dented pack of cigarettes and flicked her lighter to make sure it still had fluid, and headed for her small 4th story window overlooking the street below: Turk Street.

She stared at the ever-present white street sign hoisted above the constant shuffle of crack heads, drug dealers, and working people doing their best to avoid eye contact as they scurried to their jobs. She experienced a brief sense of delight as she imagined the horror Chao felt as he waddled down Turk to the SRO from his family's small apartment in Chinatown. The thought of him wearing his signature incognito look (Giants ball cap and cheap aviator sunglasses) to avoid being recognized on his visit to a prostitute was, admittedly, somewhat intoxicating.

That feeling went away quickly as she thought about his need for the disguise. Chao was ashamed to be associated with her. It made her feel cheap and disgusted. Worst of all, she needed him and others like him to give her life any semblance of stability. She took a deep drag of the cigarette as her mind continued to wander. She slowly exhaled the smoke from her lungs and watched it immediately vanish as a gust of wind blew through the open window. Her phone notified her of a text message. She inhaled one final drag before she put out her cigarette on the outer edge of the windowsill and glanced at her phone. As suspected, it was Chao informing her that he was almost there.

"b there soon destiny xoxoxo"

Every time a trick referred to her as Destiny, she fought off the urge to cringe. Whenever she heard it uttered, which was often, she'd have a flashback of her first time working in the neighborhood. A pimp gave her the nickname Destiny, and she could still hear his gravelly voice. "A girl like you is destined for great things; I'ma call you Destiny." It didn't matter that her real name was Suzanne Wahlz; from that day forward, everyone who knew her in the Tenderloin called her Destiny.

She walked over to her dresser to find the red low-cut tank top Chao had bought for her. Not out of the kindness of his heart, no, but because he demanded her to be naked when he got into the room without having to look at her "ugly" C-section scar and any other flaw that reminded him of her humanity. It didn't bother her as long as he paid for it, which he did, at times begrudgingly. As she slid the tank top on, she felt it was looser than usual, but she concluded it was barely noticeable. If Chao complained, so be it.

She received another text from Chao; she didn't look at it. She knew what it meant; he was there, and he wanted to be buzzed in. Patience was not one of Chao's strong suits. Almost instantly after she got the ping about the last text, he started to tap the buzzer. She pressed the intercom button, and in a faux sexy voice that poorly masked her annoyance, she said, "Come on up."

She pressed the gate button on her intercom and buzzed him into the building. A few moments later, Chao was in the room, and he wasted no time with any type of greeting.

"Destiny, get on the bed and bend over."

She acquiesced to his demands; she had to. Chao walked over to Destiny's dresser and placed his Giants cap and sunglasses in the top drawer. He then got on his knees at the foot of the bed and began to slap Destiny on her butt. "Say you like it." He said in a demanding tone. "I love it." She responded. "How much do you love it? How much do you want me to fuck you?"

She always had a hard time keeping a straight face when Chao tried to talk dirty to her. She found the idea of dirty talk cliché, and his Chinese accent made it more amusing to her. Chao stood up, undid his belt, and pulled his pants down to his knees. After standing there for few seconds, Chao asked in an exasperated voice, "Destiny, what you waiting for? Condom!" Destiny did her best version of a sexy crawl to the side of the bed, reached into her purse, and pulled out an extra-large condom. Most of the men that visited didn't need anything larger than the standard size, but the idea that someone thought they were well endowed excited them. It made the clients feel less anxious, made them finish faster, and hopefully solidified repeat visits. Destiny learned that clients didn't just pay for sex; they paid for an ego boost.

Chao grabbed the condom from Destiny and placed it on his erect penis. He paused for a moment and waited for Destiny to ask him to be inside of her. The main element of Chao's sexuality was his need to feel powerful and desired. He wanted to be treated with complete respect and subservience, or else he would become agitated. While Destiny didn't know the source of these behavioral fetishes, she understood they were there and used these observations to her advantage. Over the years of working as a prostitute in San Francisco, Destiny learned that prostitution was equal parts sex, theatre, and psychology. Comprehension of these essential components was key to survival.

Upon the first thrust, Destiny let out a moan that his 5' penis didn't quite justify. Chao sped up, and the moans became more exaggerated. This sexual dance of thrust-moan-thrust lasted for about three minutes. As he approached climax, his grip tightened on Destiny's hips to the point of slight discomfort until he let out a restrained moan upon ejaculation. Destiny tilted her head to the side and asked, "Did you cum, baby?" Chao simply nodded. In what seemed like an instant, Chao had gone to the bathroom and flushed the condom down the toilet. He did a light sink wash of his genitals and then got fully dressed. He looked almost exactly as he had before their session, ridiculous sunglasses and all, just a bit sweatier.

In a business-like fashion, Chao opened his brown leather wallet and pulled out two tattered fifty-dollar bills. As Destiny received the money, she instructed Chao to wait for a moment. She walked into the bathroom and held both bills up to the bathroom light to be sure they weren't counterfeit. "Okay, Can I go now? I have to go." Chao said in a demanding tone. Destiny replied in a calm voice after verifying the bills' authenticity. "See you later, Hun." As the door closed behind Chao, she felt a sense of relief. She had the money needed to pay her monthly fee at the SRO and just enough money left over to get what she really desired...

****

Destiny always had a slight hesitation when she was about to buy. She knew it was poison and would often fantasize about the day she would get clean. The day she would prove herself wrong. Today was not that day. She intently stared at her phone and attempted to calculate the risk of buying from one dealer over another. Her first choice was always Zach. Zach was a college student at SF State who would walk up and down Market Street, taking photos of buildings and people. He never attracted attention. Zach looked like any other college student roaming around a new city, harmlessly trying to make memories in an exciting environment before he fully set into his predetermined white-collar job and sub-urban life. He was blond, had green eyes, wore hoodies emblazoned with the SF State logo, khaki shorts, and always appeared distinctly nonthreatening and non-criminal. Despite his image, the backpack he carried contained a large textbook with the bottom half of the pages carved out to create a cavity where he stored weed, heroin, Adderall, and ecstasy. He didn't consider himself to be a drug dealer but a young entrepreneur. Zach felt his business classes couldn't compete with the experience gained by hand-to-hand sales in an unregulated market, such as drug distribution. He was a Libertarian at heart, and it meshed well with his philosophy. There was always the money, too...

Destiny sent a one-word text that read, "Henry?"

'Henry' was a code word Zach had made up for heroin. If you wanted marijuana, you'd ask for Martha. Adderall was Andy, and ecstasy was Emily. Zach would only respond if you used his code. He shied away from popularized drug slang as he deemed it could be used for evidence if he were to get caught. Now, all Destiny had to do was wait for a reply. She hated waiting.

Destiny went back to the bathroom to adjust her makeup as a way to pass the time. She thickened the dark eyeliner around the curvature of her eyes. She felt the darker and thicker the eyeliner, the more her sea-blue eyes would stand out. She was prideful of her natural beauty, but as she gazed upon her face, she silently acknowledged that this asset wouldn't last forever; even with concealer, she could still see a faint hint of crow's feet. As she aged into her 30's, she began to notice the odd gray hair or two dispersed at random throughout her naturally golden blonde hair more often. One of her fears was ending up like the old, washed-up women she would see around the neighborhood; they charged discounted rates and still ended up on the street, shaking from withdrawal. When she began as a prostitute, she felt a sense of superiority to those still working the street in their 40's. She thought she was different, but Destiny wondered if what she attributed to youthful arrogance was just internalized fear masquerading as confidence after years of stagnancy.

Nightfall approached, Destiny still hadn't received a reply from Zach. The early stages of withdrawal began to set in: minor nausea, cold sweats, dull muscle aches. She didn't want to buy from a random dealer, but she was running out of options. Destiny had roamed the streets of the Tenderloin countless times. She was familiar with all the alleyways, side streets, cracks, and crevices that made up the neighborhood. But despite her familiarity, walking the streets after dark still inspired an anxious feeling that manifested in the pit of her stomach.

Fear wasn't new to her and did little to dissuade her. Fear was just a part of life she learned to accept. She knew that there was always a chance that one of her clients could be psychotic, possibly even a murderer. She had heard horror stories from some of the other girls who work the neighborhood. Stories about men with strange demands. Men who would become violent if those demands were not met. She knew the risk she was taking every time she stuck a needle into her veins or buzzed a John up to her apartment. She felt the fear. She did it anyway.

"I'm an Irishman! Second generation in this nation! I went to the guy's house, Mark's house, I think, and they'd give me booze and drugs, whatever I wanted for free. And his wife told me to stay. And I said, 'I'm a human being, now suck my fuckin' dick!' I'm here... I EXIST!"

These were the first words Destiny heard as she exited the hotel. The man who said them was leaning against a heavily graffitied security shutter, pointing aggressively at someone or something that wasn't there. As Destiny walked by, the man muttered, "Go fuck yourself." Destiny didn't respond. She didn't look at him; she continued to walk. The further away from him, the better she felt. He smelled like death. And not in a rhetorical way. The stench that was emitting off of him was capable of conjuring a mental image of someone that had been dead for many years, and for some reason, was brought back to life for purposes unknown. Maybe he was reincarnated to let everyone know about his Irish heritage and to demand blowjobs as a right of existence. Whatever the case, the stench was so foul that it couldn't have naturally occurred due to being on the street; it required some sort of paranormal backstory to provide a proper explanation. The smell faded and was replaced with the scent of marijuana and cheap cologne as she approached three men loitering in front of a liquor store near the corner of Taylor and Turk street. One of the men looked at Destiny and asked, "You need somethin'?"

"Yeah, got any H?" She replied.

The dealer paused for a moment and said, "How much you need?"

"A bundle," she said.

"Alright, one minute. Stay here." The dealer said as he turned away from Destiny and walked around the corner. Destiny pulled a bent cigarette out of her pocket, and before she could even realize she had forgotten her lighter back in the room, one of the other men standing in front of the liquor store asked in a playful tone. "Need a light?" Destiny looked over at the man; he had a fresh tattoo of a dollar sign above his left cheekbone. She noticed the skin around the ink was still swollen. She knew not to respond. He had the aura of a pimp.

"Come on, girl, I'm just trying to be friendly. You know there's more to the city than just around here, right?

You too beautiful to be hanging out here. I can show you the finer things." Destiny continued to ignore him as she mumbled to herself, "Yep, definitely a pimp." She hated pimps. She saw them as nothing more than leeches who promised everything and delivered nothing. During her time as a prostitute, Destiny had been pimped by two different men. The first pimp she had convinced her to work in Las Vegas. He said that's where they'd strike it rich. What happened was he'd get drunk and gamble away all the money she had made. After nearly two years in Vegas, she decided enough was enough and caught the first flight back to Northern California. The second pimp was the only man she had ever fallen in love with. He was the man that introduced her to dope, he was the man that impregnated her, and he was the man that ruined her life. The dealer returned and said, "Aye, I got it." He casually walked up and handed Destiny a gram of black tar heroin. She pulled out the two crumpled 50 dollar bills she stashed in her bra and gave them to him. There was no need to conceal the exchange, as it was commonplace.

"Oh, now this bitch can miraculously hear? Fuckin' stuck-up ass dope fiend. Too good to have a conversation but not too good to shoot up dope... Fuck outta here, bitch!" The suspected pimp barked. Destiny turned and began to return to the hotel.

Along the short walk, she passed by the homeless man who had told her to fuck herself. He wasn't screaming. He was sitting against the same security shutter, clapping his hands and humming a song she didn't recognize. He seemed content. Despite his deplorable living conditions, foul stench, and lack of sanity, she found his contentedness at that moment enviable.

The withdrawal symptoms were becoming more intense. Her muscles ached, and she felt as if the inside of her stomach was disintegrating. Her hand shook as she entered the four-digit code to gain access to the building. The hotel elevator was out of service, which wasn't uncommon. The elevator served more of an aesthetic purpose than anything else. Elevators were something SRO landlords often listed as an amenity at their hotels. They never specify whether or not the elevators work. The common rationale among landlords was if the listing of an amenity equated to functionality in tenants' minds, that was their fuckin' problem.

The unique housing situation in San Francisco empowered slumlords. If you were staying at an SRO, it wasn't unreasonable to assume that you weren't in the position to complain about elevators. If a tenant didn't like it, there was always the streets; that was the mentality. The faulty elevator never bothered her until now. Her legs felt weak. What would be a casual walk upstairs had transformed into an obstacle course. She clenched the railing, taking one step at a time until she made it back to the 4th floor. The hallway was empty, and the fluorescent lighting was oppressively bright. Destiny's hands shook more violently as she gripped the room key. The sound of a door creaking open made her anxious and filled her head with memories of dread . Her fists tightened; she had been a victim before. No matter how sick she felt, she would try to defend herself.

"Everything okay, sweetie?" Asked a soft voice with an audible southern drawl.

Destiny's fists loosened. She recognized the man's voice.

"Yeah, everything is okay. I'm just kinda... sick right now. I'm uhh... need to open the door, but a bit dizzy, ya know?" Destiny replied in an exhausted tone.

"Do you have your key?"

"Yes..."

"Well, good, at least I won't have to kick the damn door down." He said warmly as he approached.

He opened the door to her room and asked, "Do you need some help? You look a little wobbly on your feet, hun."

"Yes, thanks, Terrence."

He put his arm around Destiny and helped her into the room. As he set her down on the bed, he asked, "Anything else I can do for ya?"

"Actually, there is..."

"You need somethin' from the corner store?"

"No, I... need you to help me with... something else. And if it makes you feel uncomfortable, you don't have to do it, but it would mean the world to me."

"Listen, sweetie, you're an attractive girl and all, but I like boys; ya know, with penises... "

"What? No, I know, I... I need help getting high."

"We're on the 4th story... How much higher do you really need to be? Wait, do you mean like drugs?"

"Yes."

"I don't think that's the moral thing to d-"

"Listen, I need this," Destiny interjected aggressively.

"Just because I live in Satan's asshole doesn't mean I should start breathing in his farts."

"I'll pay you."

"Well, how much?"

"Whatever you want!"

"My life leaves a lot to be desired, so how bout you say a number."

"One hundred dollars?"

"Aaaaand sold to the pretty dopehead desperately pleading on the bed! I'll only do it this once, though, okay?"

"Thank you!"

Destiny pointed to the dresser by the window and said, "In the bottom drawer, you'll find my kit. There's a belt in one of the drawers, and there should be a few lighters too. I just need you to prep for me. That's it."

Terrence walked over to retrieve the necessary items, and Destiny couldn't help but stare at the numerous deep scars that marked both of his arms. She had always known they were there but never bothered to wonder how they got there. Some of them were skin-colored. Others had a reddish hue to them as if they were infected long after the natural healing process ended.

"Okay, so what now?"

"I have some dixie cups under my sink, grab one and put some water in it."

"Why? Does heroin make you thirsty?"

"I'll explain after you do it."

"Okay, but it just sounds weird."

"It's how you do it... Just, please," Destiny replied in a soft, desperate voice.

Terrence fiddled with the bathroom faucet for a few moments before the water started to flow out of it. "Sweetie, I think your sink is bro... Oh, false alarm. It works." He filled the dixie cup to the brim and placed it on the nightstand beside Destiny's bed. With all the strength she could muster, Destiny forced herself to sit up. She wrapped the belt around her left bicep; her right arm shook more intensely as she pulled to make the belt as tight as possible.

"Terrence, I need you. Sit next to me, okay?"

Without reply, Terrence sat beside her on the bed.

Destiny laid her left arm across Terrence's lap.

"Okay, just follow my instructions. Let's not make this weirder than it has to be."

"Well, I'm helping you shoot up street heroin, and your arm is less than an inch from my penis, and I'm gay, you're a professional prostitute of the opposite sex, AND you've agreed to pay me for somethin'. I'm pretty sure we've reached the peak of the weird mountain, sweetheart." Terrence replied in a playful tone.

Destiny seemed unamused by Terrence's attempt at levity as she handed him a small baggie of black tar heroin.

"I need you to take this seriously. Don't fuck this up, okay? I'm really sick."

Terrence muttered, "Okay."

"Take everything out of the baggie and put it on the spoon."

"Okay."

"Now, open up my kit, and take out a fresh syringe."

"How do you get fresh syringes when you run out?" Terrence asked in a moment of sincere curiosity.

"There's a bunch of places around the city that give them out. How have you not heard of them? They're kinda all over the place."

"I guess syringes just haven't been on my agenda."

"You know the place where they give free AIDS tests on Market?"

"Yeah..."

"They give them out there. Anyways, put the needle in the dixie cup and pull the plunger back until it's full of water. Then push the water out slowly into the spoon until the spoon is about halfway filled with water," Destiny explained.

"After that, you put the fire at the bottom of the spoon, right?"

"Yeah, but don't just hold it in one spot. You have to move it around the bottom."

"How long do I hold the fire?" Terrence said as he flicked the lighter under the spoon.

"30 seconds, then stir it to make sure no solid bits are floatin' around. After that, heat it up for another 15 seconds or so."

"Wait, stir it with what? Is there some sort of miniature spoon I use?"

"No, just the plunger."

Terrence followed the instructions diligently.

"Make sure there are no air bubbles!"

"I'm not an idiot; I know that! I take an insulin shot before bed," Terrence snapped.

"You have diabetes?"

"Yeah, I don't like to tell anyone, though. But I feel like you can keep a secret."

"If you take insulin, then why did you ask me all those questions about how to shoot up?"

"Because insulin isn't heroin," Terrance said matter-of-factly.

"It's not that scandalous," Destiny said passively.

"Heroin or insulin?"

"Insulin."

Terrence paused for a moment, seemingly calculating the social stigmas associated with diabetes compared to heroin use. After this strange deliberation, he shook his head, seemingly in agreement. Destiny wasn't sure if he did so relative to her point or if he stumbled upon a long sought-after conclusion about the meaning of life. To her, it didn't matter. She needed to get a fix. Badly.

"It's ready," Terrence said with audible hesitation in his voice.

Destiny began to clench her fist repeatedly, and slowly, a dark green vein appeared.

She felt the pins and needles envelop her arm as the blood rushed through, partially obstructed by the tight belt. Her vein swelled, increasing its visibility.

"Now I'm ready," Destiny vocalized with the kind of exhausted enthusiasm one would expect from a soldier on their first day home from combat.

Terrence firmly placed his hand on Destiny's wrist.

"I need you to try your best not to shake. I already feel bad enough doin' this for you. I don't want to have to poke you more than once."

He slowly inserted the needle into her vein.

"Nice and steady," he whispered to himself as he pushed the plunger down.

Destiny's breaths become audible as the poison rushed through her veins, contaminating everything in its path until the eventual expulsion by the liver. The sickness was rapidly being replaced with a familiar, drowsy euphoria.

Destiny ran her hand over the patches of disfigured skin that covered Terrence's arms. He pulled back with enough aggression to signify to Destiny, even in her altered state, he didn't appreciate her treating his scars as if they were some sort of braille passage. He hated even when his lovers became too infatuated with the scars. They were painful memories manifest in physical form. They were not something you could run your hands over and interpret as a means to satisfy a fleeting curiosity.

Terrence unbuckled the belt strangling Destiny's bicep. He placed her kit on the top shelf of her dresser and began to walk towards the door.

"Hey, Terrence," Destiny said in a soft voice.

"Yes, hun," Terrence replied.

"Thanks... Can I ask you a question?"

"Sure."

"How did you get your scars?"

Terrence looked devastated by the question. His heart began to race. He had faced the question before, but he was never able to get used to it. As he opened the door to the hallway, Terrence looked back at Destiny. With a feigned smirk, he replied, "Maybe another time... "

****

The bedding was soaked from sweat as Destiny awoke from her drug-induced slumber. Her lips were dry and chapped. As she sat up, her heart began to race. The cold San Francisco air that blew through her open window brought goosebumps to her pores that worked to rid her body of the very same toxins she so desperately needed hours before. She reached for her phone to check the time and noticed that she never set her alarm. That realization came with a hint of disappointment; Destiny liked the idea of setting the alarm. It made her feel normal, like she had some semblance of control over her life. Not that she needed an alarm; the blaring car horns and roaring engines of the morning commuters' daily grind were as effective as any alarm clock could be .

She glanced at her phone to recheck the time. It was just past eight in the morning. She had three unread text messages: one from Zach, two from Herman. During her tenure as a prostitute, Destiny realized, as he became a regular, no one she had previously encountered was as outwardly strange as Herman. At times he acted like a robot, made by some sort of alien society, studying humanity, trying to live as many experiences as needed to get a sufficient amount of data to take back to his mothership for further analysis. One human characteristic Herman regularly displayed was insecurity, in between fits of jealousy.

The whole reasoning behind him seeing prostitutes was to hate-fuck them while cursing the name of his true obsession, Emily. Emily and Herman met via an online dating app. They instantly hit it off upon meeting each other, but their courtship was short-lived. Herman had a wife back home in Michigan. Emily, on the other hand, had a long line of men who were interested in her. She fed off the attention men gave her and wasn't looking for a serious relationship. She found Herman to be sweet but a bit clingy and decided to break things off. That had made Herman furious. Herman used all of his free time he had to stalk Emily's social media accounts.

He came to the Bay Area to work in the tech industry and used his expertise to monitor her online interactions. However, this made things worse. He found out she had been having casual sex with an undeniably handsome man named Ryan from Marin County. This mixture of rage and sexual energy left him with few healthy outlets to express his feelings. He did have what he would occasionally refer to as his "sweet day of revenge," where he managed to get into a house party hosted by Ryan. To Herman's surprise, he and Allen got along reasonably well. Yet, this didn't stop Herman from going into his bathroom to masturbate violently and ejaculate on a toothbrush Herman assumed belonged to Allen, all while tears streamed down his face. He thought this would make him feel better. It didn't. Realizing he couldn't keep cumming on oral hygiene products that belonged to men he didn't even know, he figured hiring a prostitute was the next logical step.

Herman's text was a picture of a man he suspected Emily was seeing. Directly under the photograph, Herman asked, "Is he better looking than me? Be honest!!!" It was typical of Herman. Destiny didn't even glance at the picture but responded, "No way! Ur way hotter." She knew he'd quickly respond.

Zach's text was as predictable as it was infuriating. "Do you still need it?" He knew she needed it. Destiny heard his voice in her head as she read the text. His cavalier tone carried over through the message. "No... I got it from someone else," She replied.

Uncharacteristically of Zach, he replied almost instantly. "From who? One of the nigs on the corner? LOL"

That reminded her of another aspect of Zach's personality she hated. The arrogance in which he spoke and his casual racism. Destiny grew up, what some would call "upper-middle class" in Northern California's Napa Valley, and people like Zach weren't anything she hadn't seen before. People born into privilege gravitate toward the alt-right because it's an easy ideology to digest. She understood where it came from and how it became pervasive. When your parents get you a BMW, but you still have to deal with the slow bureaucracy of the DMV, and you're treated like a number equal to everyone else around you, anti-government and pro-nationalist rhetoric can seem appealing because its core political goal is to let you know that you're special at the expense of everyone else. The myth of the white-ethnostate is kind of like parents who proclaim their children to be the best; even if the children keep pissing and shitting themselves at the first sign of a challenge, they're declared as better than others simply by birthright.

Zach was selling drugs, just like the men on the corner. Yet, because of circumstance, he was sure he was better. A narcotic pushing Ubermensch, if you will. It made her blood boil. Destiny didn't know if she cared for social reasons or if she just hated the idea of a college kid, who dealt drugs because it was edgy, looking down on her.

Maybe Zach's personality rubbed her the wrong way because, aside from his overt racism, she saw in him a bit of herself when she was that age. She saw the youthful arrogance, coupled with a sheltered existence in suburbia, that led her to the shitty hotel room in the shittiest part of San Francisco. A city where the poor hung from the Tree of Prosperity like car deodorizers so the rest of the world could see their existence, but obscured, in a way, to hide the noose around their necks.

Maybe she hated Zach because, aside from racism, the same youthful arrogance, coupled with the sheltered existence of suburbia, led her to the shitty hotel room she sat in, in the shittiest part of San Francisco, a city that hung the poor on their tree of prosperity; just close enough for the world to see they're allowed to exist, but far enough away to obscure the noose around their necks, holding them in place.

Every time Destiny went into Golden Gate Market, the floor was sticky. It was as if someone decided as a way to play a cruel prank on the store's owner, they'd pour soda all over the floor, let it sit for an hour, and then return to dry it with dirty bath towels so the floor would make a nauseating squelch noise anytime a customer would take a step. She walked over to the refrigerated section to grab a can of iced tea: squelch, squelch, squelch! She walked back to the counter: squelch, squelch, squelch!

"Anything else?" Asked the man behind the counter.

"Yeah, some magnums," She casually replied as she turned back to the aisle to grab the condoms. Squelch, squelch, squelch!

"Oh, I guess someone's a big boy," he said with a faux-humorous tone in an attempt to disguise how uncomfortable he was.

"They all want to feel that way, I guess," Destiny replied.

He flashed a smirk and continued to ring up her items in silence. The awkwardness made the squelches of the other customers in the store seem louder. He avoided eye contact for the rest of their interaction.

She paid and squelched back outside. She wasn't in the mood to humor the clerk. The pain in her head felt like no headache she had experienced before. It was getting worse. Her vision lacked clarity, yet she didn't feel dizzy. Her eyes seemed to possess a thin filter that robbed everything around her of its natural definition. She continued down the street, although her legs were numb. She was walking, but it felt like a glide. Her body lacked sensation; it was numb but still responding to her unconscious thought. The sidewalk acted as a conveyor belt until it couldn't. She collapsed onto the street. Her head hit the concrete hard enough for it to bounce, but there was no pain. She felt the need to get up but didn't attempt it. Something in the back of her mind told her to accept this. The pavement felt as comfortable as any bed she had ever slept on. She was tired, and this was a chance to get some rest. Her consciousness faded.

A passerby saw her collapse and called an ambulance. When paramedics arrived, they checked her pulse. She was dead before they got there. One of the paramedics, a rookie with the name Andrew stenciled on his uniform, had worked less than a month. The neighborhood could smell his inexperience.

"How long have you been a paramedic?" Asked one of the onlookers.

"This is my second week," Andrew replied with a tone that did little to mask his nerves.

"This your first dead body?"

"Yes."

"Well, don't worry, kid. There's always someone else around here to save. Maybe another time, kid! Maybe another time..."

Honest Failure

My poetry probably won't make it.

I don't have any self-empowerment mantras for the 'yass queeners'

Nor do I pretend that a change in pigmentation or gender among oppressors will equate to policy change

KQED won't like me.

My book won't make it to Oprah's club.

And the Fox News watchers already send me death threats.

Because when you write, you should write like you have nothing to lose

Even if you do.

I hope you do lose.

You should lose things.

The worst among us are the ones with the most.

If God exists, it probably hates the people who built the cathedrals far more than the people sleeping outside of them.

I know I do.

The Odds

Are we okay?

In these dark rooms

In front of these artificially illuminated screens

Even at the bottom

You get a glimpse of the bird's eye view.

Curated realities

Ingested and regurgitated

Endlessly

Swallowed and shit out again

And again

And again

The pavement may seem hard, but the dirt underneath is soft

Brittle

Like the bones of an old man

Waiting to go home.

Are we home?

Are we alone?

Are we okay?

We don't know.

Our tools improve

But our chances of an answer

Remain the same.

What to Tell a Kid

That's why you're here

I'm a cliche lucky enough to have self-awareness and a sense of humor.

Being born is a tragedy and they say comedy is tragedy remembered.

Giving birth is the first act of child abuse.

Never forget that.

Never forget you didn't ask for this.

You were just pushed into this.

You're a living, breathing trophy on someone's mantle of interpersonal relations.

This isn't your fault.

It's mine.

The world we inhabit isn't my doing, I was pushed into this, too.

You being pushed into this was my doing.

It's not all bad.

You're going to meet people and they're going to distract you from it.

You're going to laugh

And sometimes,

When those people leave, you're going to cry.

Especially if they leave against their will.

We all do, but some earlier than others.

Sometimes too early.

Those ones hurt the most.

It's normal to hurt.

If you're a man, a lot of people are going to trick you into believing it's only you that feels this.

You're not. We all do. We just lie.

Don't believe the lies meant to tear you down.

Focus on the lies meant to build you up.

The pretty lies.

Those lies are the best.

Never ask questions if insecurity is the fuel behind your search for an answer.

This is hypocritical advice.

Validation is a currency worth more than money.

And you're going to look for it.

We all do.

That's why you're here.

After all.

California Livin'

Hidden beyond the sun-drenched beaches, redwood trees
and soothing breeze

There's a yearning.

Firmly placed upon the shoulders of the modern-day peas-
ants

There's a yearning

Paradise isn't paradise.

This slice of the coast isn't yours to own, it's yours to main-
tain.

Pushed further and further away, they'll never see the day
when the breeze greets them without the fear of concrete
beds filling their minds.

Some will stay and linger; others will leave it behind.

California livin' continues its decline.

You're Not Too Big

The people

The small people

Who gather in big cities

Cities they're not from

To wear the city

Like a uniform

They add nothing

They just take from what was already there

And repurpose it

For social augmentation

Of a soul

That has no dance

If you're not from

Make sure there's a reason
Before you come
You're not too big for your suburb
You're exactly the right size.

Will to Live

Sometimes I want to die.
I'm not going to kill myself.
But sometimes,
I want to die.
I don't want to feel the fear
I don't want the rush of adrenaline
That comes with a biologically-driven
Will to live.
That sucks
I want to be somewhere distracted.
I want to be sitting at a table,
Playing on my phone
In a crowded restaurant
Or cafe
Anywhere really, and I want someone to casually walk up,
Pull out a gun
And blow my fucking brains out
From behind
I'd never see it coming.
I'd just go.
What you don't know can't hurt you.
It'd be painless
It'd be perfect.

But that's only sometimes
Other times,
I want to go hiking,
Write,
Fall in love,
Shit like that,
But sometimes
I don't.

The Cage

The cage that they've constructed.
The one that you live in
Breathe in
The one you're expected to die in
Can be unlocked
I know you don't believe me,
But it can
There is a key
All you need is for the right person...
To find it
Never let the rust on the bars
The static dimensions of the box
Or the filth that accumulates inside of it
Define your ability to grow beyond it.
I promise there's a way
You just need to find your keys.

MAYOR ALBATROSS

Victor Albatross was a man with great power and influence. He was the son of a police chief, and by the time he turned 31, he was the mayor of the town he grew up in. No one in that town was surprised by his success in local politics. Victor had been driven to succeed since he was a child and always conducted himself in a manner worthy of esteem. He wore suits in elementary school, took calculus in 8th grade, and was voted most likely to become President of The United States by his classmates in high school. Victor Albatross never failed; until he did.

Hernandez, California, the town Victor grew up in, had four distinct areas, and those four areas existed in different realities. Victor was from Fair Oaks Valley, a beautiful part of town. Lush green hills surrounded the community. The trees were tall and mature, the roads were winding, and the houses were big. Many of the Fair Oaks Valley neighborhood people had vineyards in their backyards where they would drink homemade wine and marvel at the beauty their money had bought them. One step below Fair Oaks Valley was Master Glen. Master Glen was the upper-middle-class section of town. It didn't have the rural character or rustic charm of Fair Oaks Valley, but the houses were big, and the streets were wide. Master Glen was a planned, soulless and safe subdivision. Many of its homes had 3-car-garages –

modern American suburbia. Finally, there was Downtown and Canary Flats. Downtown was poor, situated near an oil refinery, and many of the residents had, in some way, been affected by the corrosive presence of methamphetamine. Many of the residents were white, but not 401k white. They were more neck tattoo white. Canary Flats was the immigrant part of town. It was poor like Downtown, but community-oriented rather than drug-infested. Small single-family homes with flat rooftops sometimes housed as many as 10 or 12 people, but they seemed happy. The fathers went to work in pickup trucks, and the mothers sold fruit on the corner. Despite the relative calmness of the neighborhood, police still hassled them.

Victor was fascinated by poverty. He used to drive around Downtown, smell the refinery's fumes, and look at the homeless huddled under the awnings of abandoned antique shops. It made him feel powerful. One day Victor noticed a girl sitting at a bus stop. She was beautiful. Her hair was long, her body had a nice shape, and her eyes were bright. Victor pulled his car to the curb. "Need a ride?" Victor asked. The girl stared at Victor. Her bright eyes examined his brand-new luxury vehicle, and she said, "Sure." The girl got into Victor's car, and he drove toward the Marina.

No words were exchanged as Victor placed his hand between her thighs. She pushed his hand away. "What's wrong? Don't you like me?" Victor asked. "Not really, I just didn't want to pay for the bus." Victor didn't respond and continued to drive until they reached a shaded parking spot near the shoreline. The girl didn't say anything. Victor turned the car off, grabbed the girl's face, and forced a kiss. She pushed him away. This infuriated Victor. He grabbed her throat and kissed her again. She punched him. His grip around her throat tightened. She began to struggle. She struggled and struggled until she couldn't anymore. Nobody saw her at the bus stop again.

She was never seen anywhere again.

But that didn't matter because... Victor Albatross was a man with great power and influence. He was the son of a police chief, and by the time he turned 31, he was the mayor of the town he grew up in. No one in that town was surprised by his success in local politics. Victor had been driven to succeed since he was a child and always conducted himself in a manner worthy of esteem. He wore suits in elementary school, took calculus in 8th grade, and was voted most likely to become President of The United States by his classmates in high school.

And she was just a girl, sitting at a bus stop who had the terrible luck of meeting a GREAT man.

If

iF

I lived near the ocean; I would go to it every day.

I would witness the waves crash into one another endlessly.

I would let the voice in my head die.

So, my spirit could live.

I pick apart everything and everyone I encounter.

I find reasons for why they'd leave me.

I then preemptively leave before they can.

At least I do in my mind.

My body's still here

But for how long will there be anybody beside it.

iF

It wasn't

Would it bother them

Any of them

At all

Carquinez

The winds were strong.

Powerful gusts of wind rushed over the waters of San Pablo Bay.

He stood there.

He looked west toward the mountain ranges of Marin County.

He contemplated if there were any reasons left.

Any reasons left for him to consider.

The seams near the crotch of his pants tore as he hopped the barricade.

He looked down. The waves were crashing against each other.

The waters below weren't blue. The sediment carried in from the rivers that formed that Carquinez Strait altered the blue waters of San Pablo Bay into a strange brownish gray.

The fall would likely kill him...

How Much Do You Need?

How much do you need?

When the streets paved with gold

Are covered

With blood, shit and piss.

One is forced to ask

HOw much do you need?

When the toddlers that starve are destined to become pre-diabetic teenagers

And the parents are in the

'Gig economy'

Delivering nutrient-rich food they can't afford to people that won't finish their meal

One is forced to ask

HOW much do you need?

When the sick can't see doctors

And the doctors can't see patients

One is forced to ask

HOW Much do you need?

When the mantras of the oppressed are reduced to signs in the front yards owned by the beneficiaries of the oppression

One is forced to ask

HOW MUch do you need?

When the pen is mightier than the sword

But swords are made more available than the knowledge of the pen

On purpose

One is forced to ask

HOW MUCh do you need

When the image of success is constrained by new editions and monthly payments

And your life is scored on how well its managed

One is forced to ask

HOW MUCH do you need?

When walls and fences are erected to defend in the name of the invulnerable against the defenseless

One is forced to ask

HOW MUCH Do you need?

When the stability of life is based on speculation derived from the collective elite's roll of the dice

One is forced to ask

HOW MUCH DO you need?

When one genocide is bad and the other is history

One is forced to ask

HOW MUCH DO You need?

When death is coupled with debts for who have to live

One is forced to ask

HOW MUCH DO YOu need?

When tanks are utilized to evict for the sake of a portfolio

One is forced to ask

HOW MUCH DO YOU need?

When the boot straps you're criticized for not pulling yourself up by are ripped away by the same hands funded with passive income

One is forced to ask

HOW MUCH DO YOU Need?

When bombs are boring and medicine is controversial

One is forced to ask

HOW MUCH DO YOU NEed?

When the corporations are people and the people are not

One is forced to ask

HOW MUCH DO YOU NEEd?

Yet

Those in need are never asked

HOW MUCH DO YOU NEED?

I humbly suggest

That it's time

We ask.

How much should we take?

Flowers & Refinery Fumes

Polluted soil.

Cracked concrete slabs

firmly planted

On polluted soil

Refinery fumes

Lungs fit

To filter air

Changed by

Refinery fumes

Flowers do grow

In soil

Polluted

Sometimes
You just have to look beneath
the cracked concrete slabs
You'll never know
Until you do

A Train Stop Away

Daly City
And
El Cerrito
Where the bustle can be seen
But not heard
Where movement is observed
But not felt
Where fog gently caresses
The tree-lined streets
And old homes
Sit beside the new ones.
A place to think.
Peace and quiet
A refuge from the roar
High hills above the ocean
Above the bay
Where humanity's
Best and worst qualities
Are just
A train stop away

Never Negotiated

I used to wonder if my baby brother whispered in god's ear

Heaven's little negotiator

Who would've thought to place the homeless shelter beside the cemetery that contained the box designated for my brother's corpse to rot?

I used to wonder if he asked God to place me there

Because he didn't want to feel alone

Death isn't as scary when your big brother is by your side

But then I got scabies

And I saw my mom inhale methamphetamine

And the school bus made me walk down the block from the entrance of the shelter

Because parents complained to the school district

I don't blame them

They didn't want their children to see the things I saw every day.

I learned to lie.

I learned to give false addresses

I learned to take BART to the City alone

I learned how to get lost in the hopes that I'd never be found.

But they'd find me

The police would arrest me

And they'd fill me with cautionary tales

Of the horrible lives lived by adults

Who were once children that behaved like me

And over time I realized that my brother was dead

And never negotiated a fucking thing.

Vallejo, California

There's a city
That sits
Along the northeastern shore
On a body
Of water
That only flows
Through a crack in the earth
Christened with gold
In this city
Is where you find the people
Who hold the weight
Of this treasure on their shoulders
Their backs never break
And their spirits never bend
Their cup is never full
And their plate is never covered
Their contributions are never sung
But
The barriers
The bridge tolls
And the gunshots that whistle in the night
Breed a thirst an ocean couldn't quench
Welcome to Vallejo, California
Where the working class still exist

THIS WAS SUPPOSED TO BE A POEM

The world is a performance.

The outwardly radical are secretly the soft-spoken sweethearts. The preachers and other proponents of mainstream morality and principle would end your life unjustly to protect and perpetuate an idea of justice that only applies to the people without the capacity to lie efficiently with a lexicon learned at a university filled with the mantras sung by poor in the past because the impoverished in the present can't attend as they're busy mowing the professor's lawn so he can conjure new, sophisticated orations of advocacy for a class he can't comfortably maintain eye contact with in a conversation.

This was supposed to be a poem.

Caffeine Before Bed

I look longingly at things that remind me of people that aren't here.

Lights out.

Beside the glow from my phone, the room
is dark.

I'm waiting for something to happen, but nothing does.

Will it ever?

Anticipation grips me.

I need to sleep.

I took triple the recommended dose of melatonin to counter-act the caffeine.

Coffee after 5 PM is never a practical decision, but I'm not a practical person.

I'm practically not a person at all.

I'm a house plant rooted to the floorboards of a rented room on a nice street in a tough city.

Morning, noon and night hold little meaning to me.

The sun doesn't exist and the moon is inaccessible.

My time has been monopolized.

Swivel chairs and performance goals

I yawn.

Goodnight.

Tesla Couldn't Afford One

When I'm sleep deprived, the words are harder to come by.

I'll have a fully formed thought, but for some reason, it be-comes indescribable.

This inability to articulate makes me insecure

In my mind, I'm capable of perfection.

Which is a delusion.

I'm delusional.

There's no middle for me.

It's either perfect or it's shit.

And since nothing is truly perfect

My view is obscured by muddy lenses.

Muddied by my own perception of unavoidable ineptitudes

I'm smart enough to pass the tests,

But too lazy to study for them.

Because if I study

And I get one answer wrong,

I'm a failure,

But if I bullshit and still somehow manage to pass

I'm a miracle.

And that's the problem with life.

There's no more balance left.

You're either a miraculous moron or a brilliant failure

Isolated geniuses die in dark rooms

Tesla couldn't afford one.

The secret is out.

Social media ruined the PR campaign.

You're as dumb as the rest of us.

You're just smart enough to get out of bed.

Showing up is mediocrity's kryptonite

Most elites can't comprehend the words their lawyers write

They just sign their name on the dotted line

And inherit the world

While you clock in.

It's going to be a long day.

Insignificant

Art is insignificant

In a world where recognition determines value

An unknown woman writes beautifully

And dies at the hands of an abusive spouse

No one cries

No one cares

No one yass queen when she was slayed

Rupi Kaur doodles and is deafened by the world's applause

John Fante wrote better than Bukowski

Bukowski sold the books and fucked the girls

And drank the liquor and was followed by those that mis-read misanthropy as leadership

He wrote some good stuff, too.

But no one really cares about the writing.

It's the bars

The whores

The image

Not the bluebird that sung in his heart that sold the books

Not the acne scars or skid row

Not the loneliness and the musings on the pointlessness of the working class' wasted life during a 40-hour week

Make the moron feel invincible

And your bank account will be.

In order for your body of work to live

The soul has to die

Laugh all the way to the bank
With tears in your eyes

Drive-thru

I sit up in bed.
It's 5 am.
I'm going to Starbucks.
Where I will inevitably waste my time in a long line.
For the privilege
The opportunity
To waste my money
And expand my waistline.
It's hard to be a pretentious poet
When you wake up alone to coffee in the dark
And the only thing waiting for you is a long line
On the other side of town.
Drive slow.
The line will be there.
The drink will be, too.
Roll the windows down.
Feel the cool air.
You're still alive.
If you're uncomfortable,
You're still alive.
Discomfort is just a souvenir
Reminding you of your ability to breathe.
So breathe.
Feel your heartbeat.
It's there.

"Thank you for choosing Starbucks
That'll be $5.25 at the window"
You've made it
Pay for your drink.
There's nothing left.

IT GOES IN WAVES

The bluish-green hue of the Pacific Ocean always provided Caleb with a sense of calm. It was his solace. As long as the breeze cooled his skin, the World couldn't hurt him. And even if it could, he would be too transfixed by the sea's hypnosis to notice the knives digging into his delicate skin. Caleb's only wish was that one day he could go home and feel it all again. Caleb had a family. He had a brother and a sister. He also had a father and a mother, but sometimes people aren't as kind as Caleb was or as gentle as the coast he loved so much.

Caleb hated violence. His father was a violent man, and his father's violence created a weariness in him that most struggled to understand. No one knew about the demon that possessed his father. The monster that tormented his family on dark evenings. The broken bottles, blood on the bathroom floor, the hospital bills, and the concerned nurses who always suspected there was more to the story than what they had been told.

Caleb's brother Dominic was getting tired of the beatings. He was getting tired of watching his mother cover her face as best she could while the blows kept coming. And the lies that only ensured it would all happen again. He wasn't going to allow it anymore. Dominic didn't have the ocean as Caleb did. His rage couldn't be washed away by the ebb and flow of the water that surrounded their small coastal town. It remained inside. Festering.

Caleb's father returned home after a night at the Fisherman's Tavern, a local bar that he often frequented. He drove home drunk. He was mad that someone honked at him for swerving on the road. He came into the house, headed straight into the kitchen, and punched Caleb's mother in the temple while she was doing dishes. She knocked over a six-slot wooden knife block as she fell to the floor. "You fucking bitch," he screamed without reason. Dominic rushed him. They struggled. Caleb's father grabbed a knife. Caleb got in the middle of them to intervene, and that's all he remembered.

Now Caleb sits in the sand and watches the breeze move the branches on the towering redwood trees that are synonymous with Northern California. He knows the wind is moving all around him, but he can't feel it. He doesn't want to go home. So, he just sits and watches the water until he can gather the strength to face the land...

Human Nature

The tiniest speck of matter

Floating formless on a ball

Endlessly changing

Momentarily thriving

Eventually dying

To be Replaced

Selected

Naturally

Completely unaware of its existence,

Determined to continue to do so

The ones from the water

Made it to the land

Eventually standing on dry ground

Our stature grew

Literally and figuratively

There were others like us, but we, the homo sapiens, lasted.

We made the tools, claimed the land and killed the livestock

Our capacity for reasoning catapulted us atop of a food chain

We wondered why

We made gods

We went to war when we thought we were wrong

We won and lost every single time.

We fought for spirit

And died for science

Scarcity created value

The longer the duration of our dominance

The more we differentiated ourselves

Our species is special

We have iPhones and the Internet
We don't need the Amazon
We have Amazon.com
When we collectively look in the mirror
We don't see single-celled organisms
We don't see the fish
We don't see chimpanzees, monkeys or apes
We see God
We created God
But God has limits
So does the planet.
Can we see ourselves as one with the bonobos?
Can we even see ourselves as one with ourselves?
If we do, we can fix it
But only if our nature selects us to do so.

A Chance

Feel the blood move inside your idle limps.
Feel the warmth of life.
Burning.
Inside of.
You.
You sit there.
At that desk.
Your heartbeat
Filling you.
With life.
Unused.
You plan for the day.

The day you planned for.
The say when you've acquired enough.
Enough to live.
But the wind still blows.
And trees still stand.
And the blood
Is still WARM
As long as the wind still blows
Against trees that still stand.
You still stand.
A chance.

Snail In the Rain

The dirt.
The dirt is home.
Until the clouds form.
And float inland from the vastness of the Pacific.
They burst with life.
The moisture temporarily floods.
Floods our dirt.
Floods our home.
To give life another chance.
For another year.
Life is a cycle of movement.
The rain washes away the dirt
And gives birth to the slow-moving nomad.
Finding itself, appearing again.
The small vagabond.
Shell easily cracked.

Navigating a big complex world.

Planted on concrete.

We watch you from below.

Your world seems so busy.

So structured.

So Chaotic.

That you seldom see us.

Watching you.

And your chaos.

We wonder if you will ever understand

That the rain is necessary.

That you too will benefit from the fuel of the clouds.

The lubricant of new life.

Sometimes you're so absorbed in trying to avoid the rain that you don't even notice us.

You step on us.

Our shells cracked beneath your heavy, purposeful strides.

But we don't cry.

We knew the rain is the lubricant for life.

And for many to live.

Some may die.

The Sun

The heat of the sun may be too hot, but you will bear it.

The sweat of your brow may drip into your eyes and burn them, but you will bear it

The blisters on your feet may grow large and painful, but you will bear it.

Your stomach may growl and your skin may crawl, but you will bear it.

You may notice the comfortable people in their comfortable homes

Sipping cool water

With pity in their eyes

But you won't envy them.

Because if you have love in your heart

Passion in your step

And a vision driving your mind

Anything is bearable except for its absence.

Baby Hitler

Would you kill baby Hitler?

This is a commonly asked question.

Most people say "absolutely" without hesitation.

Seems simple, right?

Kill a single child and save a million children.

A worthy sacrifice.

But what if it isn't that simple?

What if we broadened that question?

What if baby Hitler wasn't really the problem?

What if the problem was the others?

The people who carried out murders

The Hitlers of the World would be powerless

If it weren't for the moral ones

who wouldn't think twice about killing something

As helpless

As a baby.

15 MINUTES IS A MUSE WITHOUT MERIT

As I sat on the concrete outside of the warehouse, the warehouse where I worked, I thought to myself, how many days have they stolen from me? The number seemed incalculable. Its scope was the only thing that felt infinite in a life where death was the only promise ever kept. How many minutes of my life could've been better utilized sitting among friends, sharing moments with people I cared for - people that cared for me. These were questions without answers. But my mind couldn't help but involuntarily ask them in the quiet moments between work. The minutes that the forefathers of our nation's labor movement fought for: breaks. Those legally mandated gaps in production prevent the worker's psyche from slipping into psychosis that I persistently longed for until the 15 minutes was finally mine. I never enjoyed the breaks.

I would spend them anxiously watching the clock as it ticked off each cyclical motion. Its constant movement designed to march me back to moving boxes for bosses whose fathers had the financial fortitude to fit their children into the universities' halls. They printed their kid's names on the paperwork that somehow granted them the capability to manage people like me.

By contrast, I am an offspring of the poor: a baby pushed out of my mothers' womb with organic lubrication,

falling onto asphalt not padded by pieces of paper present-
ing portraits of presidents. Real power can be defined by im-
ages of dead men (with no connection to your modern expe-
rience) being used to uphold a system that makes you work a
40-hour week to rent a small room while being shamed for
ingesting an avocado within its four walls.

15 minutes. FIF-FUCKING-TEEN MINUTES. To do
what exactly? I supposed it was meant for us to sit idly by
and wait for the next phase of the armed robbery I so easily
subjected myself over to. They didn't do it with guns. Well,
not directly. The schools taught these robbers a sort of so-
phistication that most won't even have enough time to com-
prehend by design. If they do, they're powerless to challenge
it in any way other than lack of participation. But that di-
lemma is for the brave, and bravery has been in short supply
among us trapped in the human condition. That was a polite
way to say that I lacked courage. Shortcomings are kinder to
the ego when spread over the collective. If I see failure in you
the same of which I see in myself, who's to say it's a failure at
all?

I checked my phone for the time. I sat there for ex-
actly 15 minutes. "Shit," I blurted out under my breath as I
rushed to my feet. I lightly jogged back into the warehouse,
where the annoyed face of my supervisor greeted me.

Supervisor: a title that implied superior vision, but he wore thick glasses, and I could see just fine.

"The break was 15 minutes, Adam," he continued, "you've been away for;" he paused to stare at the stopwatch app on his phone, "16 minutes, 13 seconds and counting."

"Sorry about that," I said, "I spaced."

"Well, you're not supposed to take more than you're given."

And that was the problem...

Expectations

Death isn't the absence of life, but the absence of expectation.

People don't cry because you passed,

They cry because you passed without fulfilling their desire.

They cry because it's expected of them.

They mourn because they expected a few more mornings with you.

They felt they were promised them.

Not by anyone in particular, but they assumed. Their subconscious promised them.

Distractions fill our daily lives.

Entertainment, gossip and hollow conversations filling mundane days

Can make the finite feel infinite.

But it's not.

And it never will be.

It's the only expectation

You can count on.

Clock In

You're in your car.

Your hands are gripping the steering wheel.

Tightly.

You clock in in ten minutes.

You stare at that tree.

That same tree that's been there.

In that parking lot.

The same parking lot that you sit in every day.

Every single day.

You feel rage building from the pit of your stomach.

It reaches your chest.

It busts out of your throat.

A violent scream.

Tears stream from your eyes.

You punch the ceiling of your car.

There's padding, so your hand isn't injured.

A minor bruise.

You take a deep breath.

And you wipe the two tears that escaped from your eyes.

Don't dwell.

Go to work.

Go.

Now.

What's Your Worth?

What's your worth?

Mine is assigned an hourly rate

I sit until

My ass goes numb

And electric jolts of pain

Vibrate

Through my idle limbs

Doing bank work

I move money.

And money moves me

To stay still

In a chair

With wheels attached to the
Bottom
So I can pretend that I
Have the option
To move
While I'm forced
To sit
Still

Futurists

The future of the world is coming.
But it's not a flying car
And it's not life on Mars
It's just one long commercial
That never seems to end
Until you do
And when you do
It won't matter
Because there's always more money
Somewhere else

Numbers & Percentages

I'm looking at math books on amazon again.
This has always held me back
Numbers
Numbers have always held me back
Percentages
And constantly being on the wrong side of them

It's never really good to be different
Not this different
Not this percentile
"You've got potential"
If I had a dollar for every time I've heard that
I wouldn't have to get better at math
I'd just hire an accountant.
He'd do things for me
I'd pay in my potential bucks
And I'd sit in my potential mansion
And get high off my own potential
Until I fucking overdose
And die
Without ever accomplishing a thing
You see -
Not being able to do something doesn't hurt that much
But almost being able to, then not being able to cut it
Is worth dying over
Over and over again
Repetition
Is the only way to get good at math...
Right?

4 Hours of Sleep

4 hours of sleep on a Monday morning feels like a knife in
the gut.
8 hours of work looming not far off in the distance
Do your best to hide the disgust in your voice.
You're so tired, aren't you

But you know restful night don't come to those that work
Restful nights come to those that take
They take the time
Your time
My time
Our time
And to them, they have all the time in the world
Which is a world with capability and promise
I know kids who've been to New York city.
I know adults who haven't
I know girls who go to Europe with their family
London, Rome, Romania and Prague
But Rome fell and London burned
Prague was occupied by Nazis
The Nazis killed the Kafkas
Franz was already dead
I don't know what happened in Romania,
but something surely did
Yet they still go.
And you don't
You're too tired
And don't have the time.

DYSMORPHIA

What is it to achieve parity? My life was one of juxtaposition. A life of contrast is prone to conflict, both internal and external. As a teenager, I was morbidly obese. At one point, more than 350 pounds hung from my suffering skeleton. I had an epiphany and slimmed down. My skeleton suffered no longer, but my skin was empty. Loose folds sat shamefully under my shirt.

To make matters worse, during my weight loss, I became strikingly handsome. My cheekbones were pronounced, my lips were thick and full, my eyes were shaped like almonds, and all of these desirable features settled symmetrically upon my face. I was both beauty and beast. All the hard workouts and counted calories that were supposed to restore my confidence only created uncertainty. I spent many nights lying awake in bed. I'd stare at the ceiling and contemplate my identity. Was I the face or the body? Was there a soul inside of me that superseded physicality, or was that just another marketing gimmick? Was the soul sold? Not by people, but to people by corporations with truckloads of T-shirts, bumper stickers, and self-help books they needed to offload on a population desperate for their weaknesses to validation by an entity other than themselves.

I was cutting tomatoes in the kitchen when it all became too much to bear. I had a sharp knife that my grandmother had recently purchased from a local salesman who went door to door giving knife demonstrations. He cut leather in half, and my grandmother was so impressed by this that she bought $200.00 worth of knives from the young salesmen who looked like he had just gotten out of high school.

I placed the knife's edge along the tip of my thumb and hesitated for a moment before making a tiny incision. A sharp stinging pain radiated from the small wound, and blood dripped down to the crease of skin between my thumb and index finger. Despite the sensation, I rubbed the wound with the tip of my finger in a circular motion, and the blood became darker and appeared thicker than it had just prior. As I grew more familiar with the wound, the pain seemed to subside. Pain is only intolerable when aided by uncertainty. If you understand the pain, it becomes routine, and its burden becomes a numbness of familiarity.

I stared at my face in the window. My transparent reflection blended in with our neighbor's home across the street. There was a Christmas tree in their window wrapped in a thin red ribbon. Red, green, silver, and gold ornaments hung from the tree with various other items. I was mesmerized by the tree. It was beautiful. No hidden ugliness existed within the tree. The ornaments were merely decorative and were there to enhance, not obscure.

I envisioned what it would feel like to take the knife and jam it directly into my stomach. I thought about bleeding out right there in my grandmother's kitchen. The sensation of my plasma settling upon the linoleum floor, but I shuddered. I wouldn't say I liked the idea that the last bit of light to exist in my dying eyes was that of the fluorescent bulbs fastened to the ceiling above me.

I sat down on the kitchen floor. I didn't want to see my face reflected in the window any longer. I didn't want to see the neighbor's well-decorated Christmas tree either. So much truth in its beauty. So many lies in mine. My face told lies that my lips wouldn't dare utter. I had to do something. Something to right this wrong. I couldn't live in limbo any longer. I thought about taking the knife and, in a quick jerking motion slitting my own throat, but death wasn't what I was after. I was after a life of truth. One that was free from burden, expectation, and stress. When your appearance is disfigured, your reputation is regarded as nothing more than an afterthought. Your saintly deeds are overlooked, and your sins are easily forgiven as the crowds rationalize the cruelty of chance as karmic retribution. The keys to freedom come in many forms.

I placed the edge of the knife against my forehead and made a small cut. Just enough to bleed. The initial sting was less severe than the cut on my finger. I stood up and stared into the window. I watched the blood follow its path down the bridge of my nose, drip onto the tip of my lips, then eventually ooze down my chin . I felt empowered. I made another incision diagonally over my left eyebrow. This one with less caution than the first. It was deeper and exceeded the pain of the initial cut on my finger, but I was enraptured at the sight of the fresh blood flowing down the curvature of my face.

I made another on my left cheek. I kept cutting in a frenzy until my pale skin became utterly crimson. Soon, my entire face was covered with slashes. I wanted to get rid of my eyebrows entirely. The pain grew intense, but I forced the blade into my skin and peeled half of my left eyebrow off. The skin just hung there with the hair still on it, thick and swollen. My hands began shaking uncontrollably, and I dropped the knife on the floor. I felt dizzy, but I wanted to continue cutting. I fell to my knees. Blood was pooling on the floor. I reached for the knife again, but it slipped between my fingers. I vomited. I was moaning in pain, but the pain was physical, and I could feel a glow in my chest. My spirit was healing. The truth was setting me free.

I lied limply on the floor. Blood and vomit surrounded me. It was on my shirt, in my hair, and plastered to my face. I managed to push myself back up. I stood for a moment, but my knees were far too weak. I couldn't stand, and I fell back down. I crawled toward the dishwasher, leaned my head against it, and began to laugh. Suddenly everything was funny to me. The glow that originated in my chest had reached my cheeks and produced a smile. The laughs were genuine and fell flatly out of my throat into the atmosphere. I cackled. The crying stopped. I heard the front door open, and I closed my eyes.

My grandmother walked into the kitchen and screamed, "Blood!" I took two aspirin that morning for a minor headache; apparently, it had thinned my blood. I bled a lot.

I was fading in and out of consciousness. My grandmother was screaming at a 911 operator. She told them someone broke into the house and attacked me.

"Grandma, it's okay," I yelled. She stared at me, and I slowly crawled toward the knife and gripped it tightly.

"What happened?" She cried.

I grabbed the knife and placed it on my half-severed eyebrow, and with a fast-slicing motion, I cut it entirely off. We both screamed. She dropped the phone on the ground.

"WHAT ARE YOU DOING?" she cried more frantically than before. I began to laugh.

"I'm finally telling the truth." After that, I completely faded away.

I awoke several hours later, handcuffed to a hospital bed. My face was wrapped tightly in gauze. A nurse was staring at me with a genuine look of sadness and concern swirling around her eyes. I looked at her, and she immediately looked away.

I was free.

Finally.

Depression Is?

Depression isn't simply a chemical imbalance

It's a society built to bring you to your knees

Depression is a landlord

Depression is a shitty job

Depression is casual sex with a person you don't know yet can see yourself hating nearly as much as you hate yourself.

Depression isn't your father's cancer

Depression is who your father was before the cancer.

Depression isn't your mother's drug addiction

Or her illiteracy

Depression is the dust caked on photos of your dead siblings in an apartment with cigarette smoke-stained walls.

It's not the loneliness

It's the inability to commit to one or the other

In crowded rooms you crave isolation

In isolation you crave crowded rooms.

Until you're just left with an undefined craving

A hunger that can't be fed.

A need that can't be met

Eventually you'll toughen up

You'll be carefree

You'll have nothing left to care about

The punches won't hurt as much.

The insults will sting less

And the ghosts of your dead dreams will only haunt you if you acknowledge their passing

You can only remember what you haven't forgotten.

And you'll eventually forget.

We all do.
Who said depression had to be so depressing?

Imperfections

A perfect conversation with an imperfect person
Is the closest thing to perfection I've ever felt.
No one really relates to the victors,
They just aspire to be them.
I admire the comfortable few
The ones that come with an overabundance of faux-pas,
And are still able to smile.
Still able to laugh.
Those are the real winners
The one who are able to analyze life with anxious eyes
But still carry the burden of existence with steady hands.
There are fewer of them than you think.
Keep 'em around, if you can.

Abe Thinks He's Something

Abe thinks he's a writer
Abe needs to make more memes
Abe is a fake Bukowski
Abe is a broke ass hater
Abe works at a bank
Abe sits in a room all day and writes
Abe wants to be alone.
Abe can't cry in front of people
Abe cries alone
Abe envisions his death

Abe can't talk about his feelings
He can only write them
Abe is weak
Abe is tall, but can't play sports
Abe hates rich people
Abe is (insert something negative)
But at least Abe is something
The problem is...
They're not anything...
At all

Trash Is a Heart Condition

Sometimes I think what I'm writing
Is trash.
And then someone says
"This is my favorite!"
And I say thank you
But inside,
I'm not thankful.
But that's okay
The pressure in my chest is building
I can feel the afib coming
And their kind words
Are what I repeat to myself
When I can't breathe.
Even if I don't believe them...

Loose Skin

The skin on my stomach doesn't look like it's mine.

It has the appearance of skin that belonged to a man who lived a long life

And died of natural causes

It looks like some kind of cruel prank

It looks like it was grafted onto my body

But that's not the case

It is very much mine.

My face is youthful.

Some have even said handsome

Although unkempt

But my body resembles a corpse

That doesn't seem to have the good sense

To realize its own death.

And maybe it is.

At least partly.

I at one point weighed 430 lbs.

I at another point weighed 219.

I have had days where death felt possible

I have had days where life felt possible, too.

And my body shows what being pulled toward both looks like.

Whether I want it to

Or not.

Abe Is a Bad Writer

Don't let doubt defeat the fire

The fire that is fueled by...

It'd be lazy to end that line with desire, wouldn't it?

Not gonna put desire

No rhyming poetry.

Not today.

I woke up this morning sad.

I wake most mornings in mourning.

Mourning what, exactly?

I don't have an answer

And even if I did, I probably wouldn't tell you.

Or maybe I would.

It's hard to determine why I wake up weighted down by disillusion

Bad things have happened, but good things have, too.

Why is it that we always dismiss the good in favor of marveling over melancholy?

Why did that line cause me to tear up?

What does that say about me subconsciously?

We're now treading into stream of consciousness territory

Which usually results in poorly written poetry.

I don't call myself Abeisabadwriter for no reason, you see?

That was a rhyme scheme.

I said no rhyming poetry.

I'm a fucking liar.

DeSiRe

Fuck.

Sincerely,

A Bad Ewriter

Diversity Tree

I have a best friend

Who has an unspoken longing

A subtle burden

A nostalgia for an experience

That never belonged to him

It's black and white

He's both.

But isn't allowed to be either.

His mother is white

His father is black

His soul is gold

And his blood is red.

But he only knows one shade

He smiles at the almosts.

Every time he sees a family that was almost his.

He smiles...

He smiles at the black father standing in front of his own home.

Tossing the ball to his son.

A ball he was never able to catch

He smiles at the hustlers guarding the stoops and the corner stores even as they size him up as a potential rival

He smiles at the Panthers holding the rifles

Aimed at the police

At precisely the same time

as the legislators aimed their pens at them

He smiles...

Through it all

He's born to be a decoration

On a white idealist's

Christmas tree of diversity

But little did they know

He'd grow taller than the tree
He was supposed to
Hang from...

NOT ENOUGH

When I awake in the middle of the night, instead of going back to sleep, I pick up my phone and, despite my better judgement, I scroll mindlessly through a sea of posts vying desperately for anyone's and everyone's attention. I then try to write, and if the words don't come, I feel worthless. I question my intelligence, talent, and ultimately, my purpose. There are few things that truly keep me tethered to any semblance of hope in an ocean of doubt.

My buoyancy is based on an assumption that beyond my many failures suggesting otherwise, that something inside of me, some ethereal source of light is bright enough to carry me through the darkness inside of my heart. This is the only thing I have. The only thing I've ever felt good at. Without it, I'm reduced to nothing. And nothing will ever be enough.

Priorities

These little words

These small notes I pour into tiny voids filled with indifference

Are the only reliable sources of solace I've never known

I need to focus more on the writing

And less on being a local celebrity

Yes... the girls send nudes

And the guys give high fives when I walk the lake.

And Silicon Valley types ask my advice

And I tell them to tell the truth

Which in their world of infinite possibility

Seems to be the only thing that's impossible for them to do

There's no app for authenticity

Venture capital has yet to find a way to monetize the human soul

Corporations admire my work from afar

Too problematic to live

Too enigmatic to die

And depending on the day

I fantasize about both

Almost

No more almost.

You know what you have to do.

Stop being so fucking scared.

No more almost.

You know what you have to do.

You know what they call almost?

Nothing.

No more almost

You know what you have to do.

The pain of almost will never leave your mind.

No more almost.

You know what you have to do

You think anyone will want to hear that story?

Of that one time,

When you almost?

No more almost

You know what you have to do

Why aren't you fucking doing it?

Don't your knees hurt from carrying the weight of your body?

Aren't your feet numb because you never ever fucking stand on them?

No more almost.

You know what you have to do.

Your heart screams it

You can see it in your mind without even trying.

That unconscious thought is your guide.

No more almost.

Almost is for the almost dead.

So, How Does This Happen?

You're standing in a grocery store

Or maybe you're in your shower

Warm water cascading down the curvature of your spine

You're staring at the wall.

You're in the moment
And then you're in the next.
Your mind isn't trying to preserve
Or expedite
And then it happens.
A surge.
You can feel it
The words
Painting a canvas
Only visible from looking within
You feel invincible
It's already written in your heart
You rush to the nearest knife
You cut a tiny incision
Not too much
Just enough to allow the blood to drip
To transcribe
To soak the paper with the essence of your heart
And your only hope
Is that it keeps beating
And blood keeps pouring

The Problem Is I Don't

You liked me better before
When I was nothing
You don't like this *new* version of me
You Don't like when I have goals
When I have drive
You don't like that I want to LIVE

Rather than just *survive.*

You remember when I was a drunk

Poor

Sick and Alone

You remember it fondly.

The problem is I don't.

Miles to Lose

Sometimes winners kiss losers

But the universe won't allow it.

It'll do whatever it can to maintain the natural order of our unnatural world.

Some things are meant to stay in place.

And you're meant to stay in yours.

Don't get pushed back a mile

Because you're trying to move forward an inch.

I don't get enough sleep.

But at least I'm not in a coma.

It's like that.

The entire fucking set up.

The winners and the losers

And why it never changes

Can be explained in the fear of lost miles

The peculiar part is

Most don't have miles to lose

Acknowledge

I, for a moment, forgot how to spell the word acknowledge

I had a mild panic attack

Any time I pause over the spelling of a word
Or the proper punctuation in a sentence
I wonder if it's all over.
I wonder if the next line won't come
If the ingredients had gone bad
If The chef has left
If The kitchen is closed
What if
The fat lady sung
And volumes of her vocal range
Were so great
That when the sound entered my ears
The sonics turned my brain to mush
And destroyed whatever writer may have lived inside
And then I remember
That the ringing in my ears
Isn't from the earth-shattering notes
Of a morbidly obese sin ʒer
But from a foundational insecurity
That on some level
believes
Any good
Even if it comes from within
Can be taken away

Gifts Get Old

On my days off I sit alone on Mare Island and
I watch the glow of the sun illuminate the waters of San
Pablo Bay as it ascends the eastern horizon.

It's just me

The derelict buildings,

The rusted bridge,

The fog horns,

The wind,

And of course, my thoughts

I aspire to greatness from the comfort of an old car.

I contemplate failure and what it means if I ultimately become one.

I envision beauty beyond the likes of which I have experienced and it envelops me.

Consumes me.

If I just write the right thing

At the right time

Maybe it could all change.

I've been told I'm talented

I've been told I have a gift,

But gifts get old.

James Franco & Lana Del Rey

You've got it all, don't you?

Good parents

Green dollars

Tattoos vague to outsiders, but meaningful to you

You know all the greats

The poets

The writer of prose

You've read the books of merit

Literary dreams

Beside bookish nights in comfortable beds

You write

But when you write

You write like the writers write.

But the source of your writing isn't the same theirs.

There's no withering in your writing.

There's no great pain when you don't do it.

And I see that in your words.

There's nothing brutal about the lines.

There's no tears on your cheeks

There's no scars on your knuckles

There's no hatred in your heart

Hatred isn't fueled by dislike

If you believe that, you've never tasted hatred or been hated

Hatred is your body's reaction to prolonged longing

Hatred is the soul's protection from sitting in a grand library at a renowned university that will never accept you because the wrong pussy pushed you out.

Hatred is the wall your mind builds while on a walk to a school bus that refuses to pick you up in front of the homeless shelter you live in because the parents don't want their kids to see what you see.

Hatred is wealth's greatest export

And poverty's miserable import that's always placed awkwardly on shoulders too weak to carry it.

But you carry it anyway.

And that's why you can't write to save your life.

Because you've never had to.

But that's okay because James Franco puts out books and so does Lana Del Rey.

CLOSE, BUT NO CIGAR

Do you think killers ever question the essence of value?

There's a housing cooperative on the western edge of Richmond, California called Atchison Village. The wartime era townhomes sit nestled under hills dotted with chemical containment tanks that belong to Chevron. A subtle reminder of who truly owned the shorelines of Contra Costa County. You can have hilly peaks blessed by ocean fog that burst though arguably the most famous gap in coastline the world has ever known, but if the owner is inclined to make a monument to toxicity, there's only so much you can do.

Roughly six miles as the bird flies from Atchison Village and the toxins perched on hilltops is Marin County - a place where the wealthy reside in a forest of their own making and the only human remnants of the sacrificed shores on the other side of the very same bay are contained in prison cells. But why? Was there any other way for people born of poverty to reside permanently in the land of prosperity beside imprisonment? Not all prisons are as explicit as San Quentin.

Fuck you, Writers' block. I was onto something.

Efficacy

Efficacy

The desired conclusion

The culmination of a dream fulfilled

Ambition to obstruct dreary realties

Nightmares lit by sunlight.

Intellect isn't a genetic trait

It's a collection of zip codes

A stack of books

Social contracts

And demanding parents.

Efficacy

A funny word used by clinicians

industrialists

Ivy leaguers

And well-read failures

The well-read failures are the worst

All the pretense

Without the ability to produce a result worthy of it.

Verbal masquerades

Mental gymnastics

And a smugness unearned

Doesn't hide the fact that efficacy is just a word you googled the definition of

But never experienced

Because if you had

I wouldn't have to hear about it.

I'd see it

During the Bush Administration

During the Bush Administration

Cuts were made.

One of the biggest cuts was to HUD.

Housing and Urban Development

Low-income housing falls under HUD.

I had an old refrigerator.

And like many old appliances, it suddenly stopped
WORKING.

The broken fridge was owned by broken people.

Who made broken systems.

To break down more people.

To keep things...

Broken

We filed a request.

We requested that HUD repair or replace the fridge.

We heard nothing.

Nothing at all.

We stored food at a neighbor's house.

She ate little.

She smoked a lot.

She allowed us to keep our food with her.

She decided one day that she didn't want our food in her
house.

She threw the food out.

After two weeks.

HUD sent an inspector.

He drove in from Sacramento.

I know, because he was annoyed at having to drive to Martinez from Sacramento.

He mentioned it three times.

He was in a hurry.

He had to pretend to fix things in Richmond.

After pretending to fix things in Martinez

For people.

People who had nothing.

He said the fridge worked.

It didn't.

He left.

A day later, my mother's social worker filed another request.

We had to store food in coolers.

HUD didn't want us to have a fridge.

I went to school.

Sometimes after school, I'd go to my friends' houses.

I'd see their working refrigerators.

I'd see their literate moms and dads.

And I'd go home, thinking about their preserved food and their smart parents.

And their living siblings.

And I'd cry.

One day, I told my friend about my fridge.

He told me it was okay and he'd help.

He stole food from his literate mother's working refrigerator.

He got in trouble.

He still did it.

He did this off and on.

For 8 months.

Until...

My mother's social worker threatened a lawsuit.
And our fridge was replaced.
I'll never forget his gesture.
His kindness.
Thank you.
I'll never turn my back on you.
I love you, Jeremy.

16th St. & Mission Station

An old man
Slacks held by suspenders
The screech of a passing train
An infant
In the arms of her mother
The remains of a pigeon
Left to rot
Pulverized by speeding metal
Made possible by bright minds
And strange numbers
And crooked men with
Beautiful
Things
And ugly hearts
The reflection of an old man in
The windows of
A passing train
The train stops
The doors open
The old man

He doesn't get on
He's waiting for something else

Refinery Corridor

Where the blueness of ocean water is made grey by oil tank-ers
And the air is cancerous
But property values are still high
Because San Francisco is close
Where the drug addicts have names
And are as likely to live in their parents' garage
As they are to live on the street
Where someone in your family is on meth
Where black drug dealers pack pistols,
Read manga,
Dream of visiting Japan
And have white friends with swastika tattoos
Who love Mac Dre more than you
Is where I call home.
Welcome to San Francisco Bay's northeastern shore
Welcome to the Carquinez Strait
A wealthy rust belt
A refinery corridor
Nothing less
Nothing more

Sophisticated Violence

Violence.
They hate violence.

But Violence...

Is the only language

That is universally understood

We may not all speak the same tongue

But we can all feel the force of a closed fist

We can all hear the explosion that propels a bullet forward

And we all can duck in the hopes that this

Hot piece of metal

Doesn't decimate our delicate flesh

How does any one person

Truly preside over another???

When something as small as the tip of your pinky

Can rip the soul from the shell that contains it

Violence.

They don't hate violence.

They hate what can't be prepared for.

The men with suits have given us an illusion

Something to believe in.

Sophistication.

Sophisticated violence is acceptable.

We can prepare for it.

We can understand it.

Or at least pretend to.

A worldly man may say to his son...

"Yes, that man is being burned alive, son, but men with expensive clothing debated it for four weeks prior to making the decision to leave this man a smoldering corpse."

"But why?"

"Because he didn't follow the rules."

"What rules?"

"The rules made by men from before. The men of yesteryear. The men with the expensive clothing of their time. The men who debated the rules for four weeks prior to coming to the conclusion that it was acceptable to burn a man alive for breaking a rule he had no say in creating."

"But why?"

"Because without those men. And their fancy clothes. Someone may burn you alive, son. And you know what the real tragedy is? They may not discuss it with anyone before-hand."

SHORELINES AND VALLEYS

I had to drive her home, but I didn't want to. I wanted her to lie beside me and watch Rick and Morty forever, but I had work in the morning, and she had a family to go home to. She wasn't pushy about me taking her home, but the longer she sat there, the more I'd want her to stay.

"Okay, let's get you home," I said.

"Oh yeah, that's right, it's 7:30, almost your bedtime, huh, Cinderella?"

"Shut the fuck up," I replied with a chuckle.

We had been casually hooking up for roughly two months. This was the first time she allowed me to take her home. She always drove to me. I viewed her allowing me to drive her home as a sign that she considered me potential relationship material. She took her time putting on her boots, and I stared at her as she tied her laces. She was short, had pale skin, dark hair, and large expressive eyes. Her eyes held a unique brilliance. She rarely verbalized her feelings. Her eyes conveyed emotions in ways words couldn't capture. It was the thing I found most beautiful about her.

As we walked to the car, there was silence. I was anxious. Whenever I liked somebody, I felt the need to transform into a jester. I wanted to make her laugh, to see her dimples deepen as she smiled. I felt good when she smiled. It made me feel as if there was something of value inside of me. I couldn't think of any jokes, so I remained silent. The house where I was renting a room sat on a hill overlooking Vallejo, California. It was a nice neighborhood in a city made famous by bad ones. I started my car and fumbled with my phone, trying to bring up Google Maps. I asked for her address, and she gave me an address in Moraga. Moraga is part of a larger sub-region in the East Bay known locally as "Lamorinda." It was an exclusive grouping of extraordinarily wealthy suburbs where the fearful beneficiaries of the Reagan era hid their money and prayed that the melanin-rich and cash poor of the nearby inner city never grew curious of what existed on the other side of the Caldecott Tunnel.

I started the car and attempted to make small talk as we drove, but my anxiety robbed me of my ability to communicate. It was so easy to talk to her before I had concrete feelings. I turned on the radio and drove recklessly to mask my anxiety. Katy Perry and static did little to relieve my nerves. I wasn't quite sure why I was so nervous. We had sexual chemistry, and when I wasn't overthinking, great social chemistry. It had to be the class difference, I told myself. For whatever reason, the women that have found me desirable have always come from wealthy families. I wasn't proud of that; it actually made me feel pretty small.

I often felt like an impostor in their presence. I spoke well, so maybe they mistook me as an equal, but I was far from it. I did everything I could to obscure my background from people, at least until they got to know me. It was especially true when it came to my interactions with the opposite sex.

The true irony was I was not too fond of the wealthy. I would often fantasize about an American equivalent to the French Revolution. I had dreams of cities burning and the bodies of oligarchs strung from trees. The capacity of my hatred for them startled me. They were people, too. Why couldn't they realize we also were people?

We crossed the Carquinez Bridge, and I stared at the C&H factory. I thought about the days that our grandparents had talked about. The days where you could get a blue-collar labor job and buy a home for your family and save what was left over to send your children to college. You'd have two kids - presumably, a boy and a girl ¬– and the boy would be a C student and barely skate by; the girl, though, would really apply herself. She would become a doctor or lawyer or something professional like that. She would achieve whatever she set her mind to; you would become a prideful parent. Maybe you didn't have the brainpower and the patience it took to read all the books she read or write all the papers she wrote, but your sweat and wherewithal bought the books she needed to read and kept the lights on so that she could read them. The problem was I wasn't my grandparents or yours, and those days have long since passed.

I could've gone over the Benicia Bridge through the Diablo Valley, but I wanted to spend more time with her, so I took the long way. San Pablo Dam Road connected Lamorinda to Richmond. She was playing on her phone, but it felt nice to have her next to me. I didn't quite understand if this was my brain responding to a flood of oxytocin or if I was in love. Either way, I felt fucking stupid. I had little to say to her, and my jokes fell flat and reeked of nervousness. Still, I wanted her next to me.

San Pablo Dam Road was lit very poorly. I was averaging around 70 MPH. The speed at which I hit the turns made her nervous. It made me nervous, too, but I wanted to seem unfazed by it. My decision to take the long way was beginning to crash against my eagerness to have her get the fuck out of my car, so I could have the full-on mental breakdown that was bubbling under the surface as a result of the strong feelings I had for her, so I sped. I loved her. Fuck. Why was this even a thing? Why does love have to ruin orgasms? Why can't we just physically feel good and go on with our miserable fucking lives?

Can our lives really be improved by someone who will inevitably spend one-third of the day sleeping, the other third at some job, and hopefully, a sliver of the leftover third beside you? Maybe conversing, maybe laughing, maybe saying nothing at all. Why were those little moments so important, and why does everything in us long for them when in actuality, our endless pursuit of those tiny treasures often made us feel worse? But yet, we can't stop. And even if we can, we never do.

After fifteen minutes of speeding in the dark, San Pablo Dam Road transformed into Camino Pablo. We made it to Orinda. West Contra Costa's smoke stacks and refinery fumes felt a world away despite only being separated by a slight stretch of backroads and rolling hills. You immediately could feel the difference - the affluence radiating from the homes. The smaller, more modest suburban tract houses were so well taken care of that they appeared to have been just built, and the larger homes bordered on palatial. Many with extravagant winding driveways and small pillars situated on both sides of wide framed doors modeled after the White House. Some were gated, and others were built on such a vast amount of acreage the paths that lead to them had street signs designating them as private roads. I began to feel sick.

Orinda and Lafayette straddled Highway 24 and had fully operational Bart Stations that connected them to a large portion of the East Bay and San Francisco. Moraga did not. Moraga was close to Orinda but lacked a freeway. You had to drive through winding foliage-dense roads to access it. Moraga was the most hidden of the three, which lent it an added layer of exclusivity.

"I can see why you were into punk rock; it looks oppressive around here," I muttered sarcastically.

"Shut up," she quickly replied with an embarrassed chuckle. "My name's Ryan, and half my personality is I live in big scary Vallejo," she quipped in a playfully mocking tone.

I laughed. I was beginning to feel a bit better. Since I was in an affluent area, I decided to blast DMX and roll my windows down just to be a prick. The air felt nice, and I began to speed again. Her large eyes widened. I wasn't nervous about the speed anymore. The idea of making some rich people momentarily nervous excited me.

"Moraga cops are bored and have nothing to do," she continued "speeding is a big deal to them."

"Oh yeah, I forgot, most cities have police departments. Vallejo has spoiled me." She smiled and rolled her eyes. I marginally slowed the car down, adjusted the decibels on DMX's barking, and rolled up the back windows.

Moraga was undeniably beautiful. Even at night, the roads looked peaceful and retained a rural character. The branches of large mature trees intertwined with sparse streetlights gave a sense of what the world could be if the march of civilization and nature came to some sort of compromise. Quite an accomplishment for a city that sat beside the bustle and bullshit that was Oakland.

She lived in a subdivision on a hill called "The Hills," complete with its own sign notifying you that you were entering "The Hills," which I found to be redundant considering the entirety of Lamorinda sat on several rolling hills, but they had to name it something. I parked the car down the block from her house so her family wouldn't see me. Her family was Arab, and despite her being 29, her conservative Muslim family would likely disown her if they found out she was spending her free time with a broke infidel. One from the other side of a bridge that her father probably helped design. She kissed me goodbye, got out of the car, and began walking toward her house. I stared at her until her body disappeared into the darkness. I sat in my car as the sadness started to build in my chest. My hands tightened around the steering wheel, and I let out a sigh. I sat there in my car for a few minutes on an idyllic street in the dark. I felt everything and nothing simultaneously. I remember her telling me in passing that her ex made a six-figure salary. My grip on the steering wheel tightened to the point of physical pain. At least I was taller than him.

I started to drive again. I had to turn the car around to head back to Vallejo. I passed her house and saw a large group of people walking around the home through the window. I saw who I assumed to be her mom wearing a hijab. I felt like I was intruding on their peaceful lives. I almost wanted to knock on the door and apologize.

I drove to Lafayette and parked my car. I began writing a long-winded text message explaining that we needed to break things off and that I would only complicate her life. I explained that the silly persona I had cultivated was a ruse to mask the dysfunction and depression that ate at me daily. I felt that I would likely complicate her life if I were to remain in it. I explained that I wasn't a likable person and that there was enough betrayal, hatred, violence, and absurdity in me to supply any given army on any given day. I started to cry. I couldn't send the message. I forgot what life was like without her. I didn't want to remember.

I got on the freeway and began to leave Lamorinda. The mid-rise office buildings of Walnut Creek glowed in the distance. My brain kept playing back her telling me about her ex's income. It felt like I got hit by a bus. I screamed "fuck" at the top of my lungs; I didn't hate the rich. I only hated myself.

I had work in the morning. It was already late, so I decided that was a justification to go 100 mph. I flew out of Walnut Creek into Concord; Concord quickly turned into Martinez, and the nostalgic smell of refinery fumes entered my nostrils. The odor produced by not one, not two, but three refineries situated in a sort of triangle around the Benicia Bridge was horrid but strangely comforting. I stared at the lights of the oil tankers that flickered on the waters of the Carquinez Strait as the bridge led me into Solano County. Benicia flashed by and turned into Vallejo.

I was finally home. I decided to go to a fast-food drive-thru on Tennessee Street just a few blocks from my house. I was sad, so I wanted to fill my body with trash. I promised myself that after this last binge, I would start taking my diet more seriously. Deep down, I knew I was full of shit. The line was long, almost too long. I clearly wasn't the only person who hated themselves in Vallejo. That's what I loved about Vallejo. It was a rustbelt, almost midwestern American dystopia with a Filipino flair that had the awkward luck of touching the same bay surrounding San Francisco, which did nothing for Vallejo except for further its own embarrassment. There were also rappers in Vallejo. Surprisingly, many of them rapped well. So there was that.

After what felt like an eternity, I finally made it to the drive-thru window and was handed a greasy bag of dogshit that had so much weight to it that I immediately began to realize I didn't need to spend $30 on Jack-In-The-Box. Despite the lack of necessity, I would consume it - all of it, in one sitting. In my bedroom. Alone.

I pulled up to my house and considered eating in the car. The last thing I wanted my landlady to see was me walk into the house with what resembled a full-size brown paper grocery bag of Jack-In-The-Box. I looked behind me and found an actual grocery bag with a real grocery store's logo on it and put the greasy bag in it. As I walked up the drive-way, I started laughing at my stupidity.

After eating my mountain of heart disease, I looked at my phone and deleted the message saying we should call it off. I told her I made it home safely and sent a heart emoji.

I lied in bed and thought about the day. I came to three solid conclusions: I loved her. I was terrified of love... And I ate way too much Jack-In-The-Box.

Manifest

Can the mind manifest?

I hope it can

Because in mine

I can see you planting tomatoes in our garden

We'd have a modest home near the coast

Shrouded in morning fog

Basking in the afternoon sun

And settling in the chilly night air.

I can hear noisy stairs that creak with the sound of a well-loved residence

Lived in by many others

And this time it'd be our turn.

We'd drive downtown

Go shopping

And you'd hold my hand

Or more accurately, my thumb

As my hand is much larger than yours.

And things would be okay.

And life wouldn't hurt so much

And you wouldn't cry anymore about being a woman

Because it wouldn't inhibit you

And the traumas of poverty wouldn't burden me

And the streets wouldn't smell like piss

The air would be fresh

Filled with the smell of food and other pleasantries

The graffiti on the walls would be genuinely hopefully

Because we'd be in a place where hope didn't feel like a waste

Most of my writing is dark

But I genuinely don't want it to be that way
Forever.

Beautiful Eyes in the Valley of Prosperity

On the southern tip
of the waters that flow
from the golden gate
You'll find it:
The valley of prosperity
The Wall Street of high-speed internet
The Hollywood of high GPAs.
Home to the semiconductor,
Google
And a guy named Steve who created a lot of jobs
But more importantly
Home to her
The one with the beautiful eyes.
She reads
With a bookshelf filled in with leather bound editions
She writes
With a fervor
And recites
With a fervor contained
Deep breaths punctuate the end of each sentence
Her heart rate rises with each rendition
There's something in the way she struggles through her
words.
But her struggle doesn't take away their ability to dance.
To treat the page as a ballroom for her pain to be notarized

And hopefully one day
Verbalized
She speaks with the pain of the chronically misunderstood
And all I want to do
Is to
Understand.
Her.

Imagination

I imagine a life with you.

We would walk in the forest together

And fill our lungs with clean air, free from the toxicity of humanity's unchecked progression.

We'd take slow drives in the fog.

Glide past giants as the road curves.

Hold my hand when you need it.

I imagine a death with you.

After a life that feels completed

But that's only in my imagination for now.

When the City Slows Down

You drove 5 hours.

5 hours from the solitude of California's forgotten shores

To the bustling lights of a loud city on a quiet Saturday

San Francisco is a fast place.

Filled with fast people.

That do fast things.

It moves so fast that most aren't fast enough and get left behind.

Left behind, only to witness the glow of the fast and beautiful city fade into obscurity.

On a cool Sunday, the city seemed to slow down.

It seemed to slow down for you.

It seemed to slow down for me.

We met near a bookstore, near a city light that shined bright despite being completely surrounded by things that glow.

It still shined brighter.

I showed you the palace of the poets, thinkers and writers who had the ability to provide clarity in a city known for fog.

I showed you where the immigrants find their slice of home in a land of runaways.

I showed you the highest hills.

The hills where the rich people live so they can be closer to the Gods.

The Gods hate them.

I hate them, too.

And we laughed.

We laughed the whole way.

The screech of the train isn't so loud when I'm with you

The human excrement isn't so depressing when I'm with you.

The shackles feel loose and the city feels slow when I'm with you.

I took you to the alley where the spirits of the forgotten are contained.

I bought you a burrito.

I bought myself one, too.

I enjoyed every bite.

I looked into your eyes and they were blue with a slight greenish hue, nearly matching the color of the water that surrounded us.

We walked.

And we laughed.

We made it to your car.

You gave me a book.

I gave you a kiss.

And then we drove.

We took left turns.

We made it to the top.

We laughed the whole way.

And then we embraced.

I stood there and I held you.

The fast city stood still for a few moments longer

We kissed.

You said goodbye.

And the City became fast again...

Taking Back Sunday is Also the Name of a Band, At Least That's What I've Heard

Take me back to Sunday.

Take me back.

Take me to where I drove 2 hours to be

On the western edge of the earth

Where it meets the sea

I want to feel the Pacific Ocean's breeze.

I want to feel your arms around me.

By the mossy-green redwood trees

And the museum
And the bored men playing golf.
My heart was beating hard
But your embrace was warm and soft
I couldn't fucking breathe
But I didn't need to
Because I was there
With you.

Comfort Zone

You're not my comfort zone
You're a manifestation of my fear
You're a piece of my potential
My potential life
My potential partner
You're what could be
You're what can be
If I hadn't spent so much of my life
Divorced from that very potential
But I don't want to be defined
By missing bullets
Lightning that almost strikes
But always struck out
I want to uncomfortable
I want to be uncomfortable
With you.

Floor

I want to lie on your floor

In your apartment by the ocean

I want to be eye level with the dust particles

that accumulate on your carpet

I want to watch documentaries about places I've never been

I want to paint the walls of your living room black

And the windows that let the world in white

Because darkness is only romantic when it's transitional

Light is where life lives

But the sun isn't unique enough for you

And the windows aren't good enough

And the door won't close correctly

And the toilet is always fucking clogged

And the dishes are always dirty

And the walls...

Who painted them black?

And what kind of moron would paint windows at all?

Are you trying to block out the sun?

Do you think you're bright enough to compete with the sun?

The warmth of the burning star is only soothing when
you're not on fire.

Lie on the floor with me.

I'll explain.

TOKYO BUCKET

The neon lights of modern Tokyo have a way of making you nostalgic for the future. It doesn't feel real. As you step off the plane, you are instantly propelled into some sort of warp. A paradigm speeding forward and backward in time simultaneously, and all you can do is hang on and try to process it. The environment was so loud, but the people were so quiet. Bright lights shined brilliantly on the surfaces of eyes that darted between various sources of stimuli and avoided contact. The well-dressed men looked tired; the poorly dressed men looked tired in a completely different way. The women looked content but anxious. There was an immense tension filling the air that counter-intuitively produced an eerie calming effect.

I took the train to a downtown district called Chuo City. Faces came from every direction. Signs were in a mixture of English and Japanese. There was a man on the sidewalk, standing on a bucket screaming into a megaphone. People seemed to go out of their way not to notice him. The louder he shouted, the less they could hear. They were busy with everything and nothing. Men sat in smoke-filled bars laughing amongst themselves. Women walked quickly through the crowd. Children flooded into arcades. Police officers stood planted on street corners, scanning for those that didn't fit. The bucket man didn't fit, but he was accounted for. He screamed louder. His eyes filled with tears. I looked at him. He looked at me and shouted. His loud yells became strained cries. He stepped off of the bucket he was standing on and walked toward me. He placed his hand on my shoulder and lowered his megaphone. He cried to me in Japanese, but I didn't understand anything that came out of his mouth. He made me anxious. I brushed his hand off of me and walked faster. He followed me. I tried to lose him in the crowd, but he was able to keep up.

I turned into a clothing store and rushed into an unoccupied fitting room. I sat there for an hour, thinking about the man on the bucket with the megaphone. How starved for attention, he must have been. He didn't speak English, and I didn't speak Japanese. No meaningful communication was likely to occur between us, but I felt that he needed to connect with me. He needed my confirmation. He needed proof that he still existed. I heard a loud banging on the door. An employee for the store instructed me in heavily accented English that I needed to get out of the fitting room. I smiled and nodded and began to walk outside. I didn't know what else to do and decided it was time to head back to my hotel. I once again boarded the loud train filled with quiet people.

I made it back to the hotel I was staying in a historic district. There were temples and parks of significant size. It was still relatively crowded, but it was by no estimation bustling. The buildings were low rise residential dwellings. My hotel was modest in comparison to the steel behemoths that towered over the central city. I pulled out my wallet to retrieve my keycard and opened the door. As the door swung shut behind me, I felt a sudden illness spread across my intestines, filling my stomach with a violent acidity. I turned on the light, and to my shock, there he was... He was in the middle of the room. He was standing on the bucket. His eyes were still moist with tears. He raised his megaphone and appeared to scream, but I couldn't hear him.

I couldn't hear anything.

The Sky

I was blessed with height in a world determined to make me feel small

Aspirations remained as low as my stature was high

I grew into a façade

I look exactly like everything I'm not.

As a result

Belonging remains stubbornly out of reach

My family is almost gone.

I watch the sands of the hourglass chip away at their existence

And realize I'm on the verge of existing alone.

And then the loneliness takes hold

Envelops me in ways it only can

And I sit with it

Lie with it in my room

Eyes pointed toward the ceiling

But I can see the sky.

I can still see the sky.

Dystopia On Pause

The grinding gears have come to a complete halt

The mechanisms of capital struggle to breathe

As fascists storm the Capitol

We watch a nation dying of a new pneumonia

The rents fall as the bodies drop

Dystopia on pause.

The monuments of wealth lie empty on once bustling streets.

The coastal elite can drown in the same waters they appear to walk on

There's no right way to watch a corpse wither

Only advice from people who don't know death.

They've only studied it, but never shook its hand.

So, we wait for a hero that won't come

Because prophets only keep promises that are profitable.

The Edges & the Middle

Artistic expression has always sat on the edges of the class spectrum

The excessively rich recline comfortably in dense urban apartments or spacious suburban

estates and produce art with an ease of mind that comes with abundance.

The desperately poor have an abundance of an entirely different kind.

An abundance of time with little at stake if they fail

The winners have it all

And the losers have nothing

Yet both are blessed with the ability to create

It's the people in the middle

The people still stuck in the game

Too much to lose

Too much to gain

No spontaneity

Lives spent structured and gutless

Fear and consumption

Credit cards and debt collectors

Checkbooks balanced by the chemically imbalanced

Words remain unwritten and unsaid

Paintings fade from the mind before the brush can touch the canvas

Guitars sit out of tune in dusty garages or cluttered bedrooms

Waiting for a weekend that'll never come

Art sits at the edges

Because there's nowhere to sit in the middle.

Never Drink Good Coffee

If I could give you one piece of advice that would reduce frustration and disappointment in your life, it would be this: Don't get used to expensive coffee. Good, single-source roasts will inevitably ruin your life. Embrace garbage coffee.

Every morning should start with a cup of stale Folgers coffee and a stranger slapping you in the face.

The remainder of the day is likely to be an improvement.

Only read and consume bad news.

You may not be paid enough at work, but you're not in Somalia.

Remember Somalia, Iraq and Flint, Michigan.

Remember it's worse than the traffic.

Drink the shitty coffee.

You'll learn to like it.

Never drink good coffee.

It's all downhill from there.

Empty Lot During an Election Year

Empty plots of land
Surrounded by homes and businesses
In the vastness of suburbia
Dirt undisturbed by developers, contractors and construction workers
Waiting to be sold
Land parcel purgatory
Temporary placeholders for people without places
Beside signs with pictures of men in suits
Promising changes to things undefined
I guess it takes a man in a suit
To clean up a mess made by other men in suits
And the city burns.
But the land remains for sale.

They Say

They say "I'm here for a good time, not a long time."
They say "die young, leave a beautiful corpse."
But I don't believe them.
I've been in the shelters.
I've been in section 8 housing.
I've seen how people can make a short time feel long.
And they don't look beautiful at all.
When they die.

I Left My Heart in... El Cerrito?

I remember going on hikes in Wildcat Canyon, a bright spot nestled in the gloom of Richmond, California.

I remember slow drives on Arlington, a scenic route to BART.

When you see the blue sign that welcomed you to El Cerrito, the nice homes on Arlington get even nicer.

You look down the hill, you can see everything. Yet you see nothing.

I remember the seagulls that perpetually circle the sky above

I remember the steam that rose from the towering pipes of the Chevron refinery.

I remember the novelty of the Albany Hill.

"What a strange hill," I'd say to myself.

Then I remember smiling.

I remember sitting alone in my car on the very top of the parking structure at BART, daydreaming that one day, I'd never have to leave this spot. I'd sit there and feel content in the delusion of solitude. I could see them, but they couldn't see me. And in that moment, I'd feel what I imagine it is to be free.

THE ATLANTIC

I'm tired and uninspired this morning. I feel like I have nothing to say that hasn't already been said by a million other writers in a million different ways with phrasing better than my own.

I have a headache and I'm tired and my stomach hurts from overeating last night. I likely consumed anywhere between four and five thousand calories. Now I'm not going to eat anything for the next twenty to forty hours in an attempt to reset my guilt before the next three days of healthy eating that will likely lead to a fourth day binge and fifth day fasting period.

I sent a short story to *The Atlantic*. I know they won't read it. And if they do read it, they won't publish it. And if they do publish it, it wouldn't change much. It's a story about a man thinking about how our breaks from work are often spent dreading going back to work. It's about how most of us live our lives in a constant state of dread while the people who own us dominate the art inspired by the misery that they've created. Then they look out of their windows, look at the beautiful earth that they've inherited and somehow still feel empty, yet superior. These people are generally who would read something like *The Atlantic* or *The New Yorker* or any other random literary magazine I read as a kid. I used to hold these magazines in high regard, but I've come to realize that behind the beautiful words lies ugly inaction. They read stories about the poor in America or the extremely poor in other parts of the world and they read with enjoyment, sometimes a tear or two slips from their eyes as they feel sympathetic to the plight of the people that exist on meager means in the narrow space carved out for them between the surface of the publicly funded concrete and the privatized plastic sole on the bottom of their boot.

And just like that, I've found the cure to writers' block. All you need is caffeine and silence.

Time to pour another cup.

Traffic Lights

The traffic lights.

They're always there.

Stop.

Go.

The most interesting traffic light is yellow.

It's the most daring traffic light.

It's an inquisitive light.

It's asking...

"Are you gonna do it?"

You can stop, but are you?

The yellow light forces us to confront ourselves.

How you react to the yellow light is likely how you'll live your life.

You can abruptly stop.

Jerking forward as the brakes force your vehicle into stillness

Or you can risk a crash.

But if you don't crash.

You may just get to where you're going.

On time.

Art Is?

Art is...

More.

It is more than expression.

It is an individualized searchlight

Cast by the

Fire

In your soul.

In the hopes.

That its *gLoW*

Will find someone

That someone.

Will understand.

And they will understand.

Because it's the only thing we've ever

Under

Stood.

Write for People

I don't write for writers.

I write for people.

Anyone can *technically* write.

But most writers are derivative

They write like they read a lot of writers

But they don't write like they've experienced anything worth writing about.

I don't care about your cool autumn mornings in your small town in the Midwest.

I don't care about how many large words you can use to describe a sunset at dusk and how you're going to predictably segue to a metaphor about love or death.

I

Don't care.

If you've left your small town because you thought that you were too talented, too big to be there

You have no understanding

That bright lights shining from big buildings

Towering over humanity

Won't mean a thing when your soul is dark and your passion is an aesthetic choice.

You're not going to be young forever.

Why waste time?

I've Read the *New Yorker*, Too

The written word has been hijacked by hyperbole

Misused by miscreants whose muse is nothing more than their own reflection in the mirror hanging on walls littered with photos of writers who they have never read

The universities are filled with dullards who never doubt their capabilities because security has filled their soul with self-belief and life has placed bag filled with books of daily affirmations to distract from the fact that this is a planet and they're organic matter on a ball being lightly toasted to eventual oblivion by the star they're so desperately trying to become...

And that's why you shouldn't write

Unless you should

No Time to Eat the Rich When You're Starving

Artists live in poor parts of town and make art critical of the rich for the rich to consume.

The cycle of life.

And death.

The working class don't have time to sit and read or observe the creativity their struggles produce, because if they did, they might slit your fucking throat.

They have to sleep and get to work.

And work harder

So, they have a place to spend their time.
Sleeping.
But always tired

Words

The human ego is an incredible specimen.
The way it can warp words and conflate meaning
The structure and restructuring of organized noise.
Beautiful sound
Curated by the same 26 symbols.
Used to convey, despite its limitations - the full spectrum
Of what it feels like to be alive.

Boring

"Poetry should never be boring"
            -Charles Bukowski
The written word, literature, prose...
Whatever you want to call it
Has been hijacked by people who write with their minds, not
with their hearts.
They think that because they were depressed makes them
an artist.
These people.
With their parents
Their parents... who love them
And believe in them
Instilled in them a belief in themselves
That they're good enough
Fools

All of them
Will end up
Editing
But never
Writing.

Zoomers

Zoom calls,
Riots,
Working in your underwear,
Hand sanitizer,
Facial masks
And Fascism.
Welcome to the 20s.
Enjoy your new decade.
You deserve it.
At least I hope you do.
And if you don't
At least you have $1200.
And if you haven't gotten it yet...
You can always loot a Target.
Because in a world where
Cops are killing with impunity
And a new virus literally drowns you
Either physically
Or economically
Sometimes
You need a new PS4
For free

To make you feel like you've gained something.

In a world that's on the verge

Of losing everything.

TO GAIN

"The rich want you dead!" he screamed to anyone that would listen.

"The food is poison and they don't care," he continued, "They want your children so they can work them to death and feed them poison."

He stood there, pointing wildly. Directly behind him a fluorescent lightbulb flickered dramatically. The flashing made his shadow appear demonic. My mother's grip around my hand tightened as we approached the screaming man. He was wearing a dirty camo jacket. It wasn't the usual earthy-green, but a mixture of white, silver, gray and black. The jacket was filthy, but fit him well. His pants were dirty, too. But unlike his jacket, they were much too big. The pants must have belonged to a man who weighed over 500 lbs. He didn't have a belt; the pants were fastened to his waist by an electrical cord. Our eyes met.

"THEY'RE GONNA KILL. THEY WILL. THOSE RICH BASTARDS WILL GET YOU SOONER OR LATER!"

I looked away. A BART officer approached the screaming man. The man continued to scream, "they'll kill you; they'll kill all of you!" He looked at the BART officer and dropped to his knees. "Put your hands behind your back!" The officer demanded. The man's screams became unintelligible mutters. The officer pulled the man to his feet and took him away. As we approached the steps leading to Market Street, I looked up at my mom and asked, "Are we poor?"

"Yes," she said.

"Do the rich want us dead?"

"I don't think so. They're already rich. What do they have to gain?"

What do they have to gain?

Men With Guns

Don't fear the men with guns
They're scared.
That's why they have guns.
And stand in groups.
A gun is an admission of vulnerability
Cloaked in a veil of power
A group is needed for those who can't
Stand alone
Don't fear the mean mugs.
They cry, too.
Fear the men with pens
They're not scared
They stand in suits
They control the men with the guns
And they never cry
For you.

A Thousand Deaths

They say a coward dies a thousand deaths
but brave men only die once
I assume they're talking about rich brave men
because there's plenty of poor brave men who die every single day
just so they can keep living under a roof

Invulnerability

Money isn't the root of all evil.

Invulnerability is.

Which is a commodity that can be bought.

A lifetime of cheekbones untouched by knuckles

Can make monsters out of otherwise average men.

Most men are average

Most women are, too.

Circumstance is a masquerade

That allows a few to wear greatness like a costume

And many to bear the brunt of failure like a mark

Nooses tied around the necks of infants

Should never be blamed on the prior choices

of poorly equipped parents

Blame the manufacturer

Who made rope that can knot so easily

Around the throat of a child

George W. Bush Paints Now

There's a holocaust in the heart of every human being.

Behind the veneer of civility lies a creature whose cruelty could kill.

You just have to find the root of their hatred.

Once found, the right selection of words can fertilize the soil

Strengthening the tree of their disillusion

Strong enough to hang the bodies - carry the bodies

Without breaking the branches.

Everyone carries a clenched fist for the face guilty of their failures

As long as that face isn't their own.

The thirst for blood is best quenched by the flavor of the unfamiliar

Homicide is only murder if forced to attend the funeral
And strangers aren't invited to those.
George W. Bush danced with Ellen.
He killed a million people.
He paints now.
I've heard he's pretty good.

A Small Room with Dirty Windows

When I was young, I was a truant.
Anything that reeked of responsibility was met with re-
sistance
I would rather sit in small rooms
With dirty windows
And warm Xboxes
And stale soda
And air that was tainted with thick cigarette smoke.
There were no presidents in that room
No politicians
No morticians either
No God
No devil
No life
No death
Just dust
My own collection of debris
I'm not made for this thing here.
I'm made for that room.
That promise of perpetual solitude

That freedom from the world lying in wait on the other side of that dirty window that I seldom looked out of.

There was nothing I needed out there

That couldn't fit in my dirty room

That somehow felt cleaner

Then anything I've encountered outside of it.

The Wrong Kind of Love

There's a syringe filled with heroin being injected just a few blocks from where a privileged child is taking his first of what will be many piano lessons. The love and warmth expressed in his mother's eyes as she watched her only son's tiny fingers touch the keys was exactly what the addict was attempting to buy:

Love.

The unconditional kind.

The kind of love that turned rain clouds into green foliage.

The kind of that inspired the dark arts and the beautiful deaths

The kind of love you'd pay to kill yourself for.

Like a good mother, the high doesn't judge.

The average passerby may, but they're just addicted to the acceptable addictions.

Food, fucking, caffeine and capitalism

It's okay to be a self-destruction fiend as long as it benefits the fiefdom.

You know that.

You can hoard wealth and be called a hero

But you inject a chemical that can turn the damp concrete on the forgotten corners of the metropolitan wasteland into a comfortable bed and you're a monster.

But your brokenness isn't their concern

And your sickness isn't the issue.

You're just the wrong kind of tired.

You're just the wrong kind of sick.

You just want the wrong kind of love

Guy Fieri is an American Treasure

The diamond.

Floating in a sea of garbage

Perpetually sinking

Unidentified among used food wrappers,

Diapers filled with baby shit and all the things we bought, but never used.

A world of antiquated dust collectors that take up space in garages beside the cars that take us places, but get us nowhere.

Floating in this.

Floating because of this.

Never able to breathe

But unwilling to drown

Hi, I'm Guy Fieri.

You're watching Diners, Drive-ins, and Dives.

Welcome to Flavortown

What the fuck, America.

I DON'T KNOW WHY I WRITE LIKE THIS

I don't know why I write like this. How is it that every written word falling onto this faded keyboard feels so heavy and burdened? It's like there's two people inside of me. There's Abe and there's this *other* - a seething entity that is entirely a part of me, but completely detached from my consciousness. My mind often goes blank when I'm writing. There's pauses where I rethink lines, but the best writing occurs when my mind is silent and this phantom driver takes hold.

Emotions will spring up and I'll mourn things I didn't know made me sad. I'll think about the old man sitting at a bus stop in his stained work uniform and hate the world for him. I'll envision his boss being gripped by the throat and beaten for every opportunity lost and dollar stolen. And mourn the fact that he doesn't have the guts to do it. I'll think about an accountant for the NRA being assassinated by the mother of a young child killed in Chicago with the very same gun that took her son. And then my mind will shift to other things. I'll think about photos of Sylvia Plath and wonder why I can't stare at them for more than a few seconds without feeling uneasy - her images don't feel static. They look like they're aware of you. Maybe they are.

Winter

I want it to remain winter forever
I want to live a life of low visibility
I want the fog to reduce you down to your silhouette.
Neutrality's natural ally has always been obscurity.
Please don't tell me more.
I want to feel less.
There's no power in knowledge.
Ignorance is bliss
I want to ignore you.
All of you.
Space is everywhere
The galaxy perpetually expanding
Yet I can't get far away enough.
No peaceful port appears
Because I take you with me.
Haven't you taken enough?

This Won't Last Forever

A fiery orange gripped the sky.
Moist dew accumulates on lush greenery
Concrete damp with remnants of a passing night.
Pebbles and dog shit
Grass and tire marks
Homes
Some owned by those who reside
Others owned by those who invest
Cars:

Some parked

Others in motion.

The apex predator of suburbia.

Noise and exhaust

Noise and exhaust.

Exhausted by the noise.

This won't last forever.

You know?

The Little Wins

When someone contemplates suicide

Their mind tends to be absorbed with

The big losses

Rather than

The little wins.

Yes, someone may have died

Or your wife left you

Or your friend betrayed you

But...

You did like that sandwich

And there's that song that made exercise feel effortless

And on the train.

A child smiled at you

For absolutely no reason.

Other than the fact that seeing you alive

Genuinely made them happy enough to smile

So...

Maybe there isn't some big, important reason to continue living

But...
There could be a million small ones you're overlooking

Canvas

My body is a canvas
Displaying the art of self-destruction
In every loose fold
Lies a perfect brushstroke
A touch of ambivalence and self-hatred
American poverty's nutrient deficient excess
Absorbs my skeleton
Envelops my heart
And displays the weakness in my soul.
When I look in the mirror
I can't help by marvel
At all the death
I've managed to survive.

Writer's Block

I've never struggled with writers' block until people started to call me a writer with a tone indicative of sincerity.

The more they did it, the more I felt I had to live up to it.

To their expectation of what I am or their perception of what a writer is.

I was willing to write as much as I needed to keep their attention focused on the flowery words that flowed from my fingers like blood from slit wrists onto bathroom floors during those desperate days when time erodes righteous fury into perpetual fatigue.

I never had to fit into a box until I desperately forced myself into one.

The faucet never turned off until I began to question who was paying the water bill.

Capitalism is the natural enemy of spontaneity.

Don't try, but never quit is the mantra of an artist.

The moment you start trying, is precisely when you should quit.

The paintbrush will lose its ability to convey colors with the brilliance they once held.

Words will lose the meaning you once were able to give them and ultimately be subjected to the indifference of dictionaries.

There's a word for that, you know?

Death

Irregular Thoughts

Irregular thoughts
Are usually the ones that resonate the most.
In your irregularities is where you find your truth.
Greatness isn't common.
If it was, it wouldn't be great.
If you're not being ridiculed, you're not on the right path.
Pretending won't do it.
Posturing for applause is the quickest way to fade into obscurity.
They can smell it.
They can smell the inauthentic.
You can't buy it.
You just have to be it.
You can say it.

But it's not what you say, it's how.
And you've never known how.

NOSTALGIA

I was just released from prison. The Powers-That-Be let me out of San Quentin, and it was the first time since 1992 that I felt the breeze come off the shores of San Francisco Bay on the right side of the barbed wire fence. I needed to go back to Oakland. All I knew was Oakland. On the way out, a CO gave me a blue plastic card with the word "clipper" written on it. He said there was $20.00 on it and told me to "get the fuck out of Marin, and stay out." A bus stop was not far from the prison's gate; I stood there and waited for something to happen.

The wind felt good; I liked the wind. It was an overcast day; I liked it like that. My cell had a window, and during hard torrential rains, I could hear the water hit the window, and it reminded me that there was a world outside of these walls. These cells. That prison.

A bus eventually pulled up. I got on, showed the bus driver my blue card, and began to walk toward the back of the bus. "Excuse me, sir," he said. I looked back at him.

"What?"

"You have to tap the card on the scanner." I walked back toward the front of the bus and asked, "can you show me?" I handed him my blue card, he tapped it on the scanner and gave it back. "Is this bus going to Oakland?" I asked. He looked at me with indifference and said, "No, this bus is going to the San Rafael transit terminal, there you'll be able to get on the 40. That will take you to the El Cerrito BART Station."

He handed me back my bus card, and I walked past a few rows of empty seats. I sat down and leaned my head against the window, and enjoyed the ride. I saw Mt. Tam, and it was gorgeous. Freedom had a way of enhancing beauty. Water became bluer, trees greener, the air sweeter. The bus went over a bridge. The Richmond-San Rafael bridge crosses just south of the San Pablo Strait — a narrowing of the water that separates San Francisco and San Pablo Bays. They all looked the same to me. Beautiful. I saw the cranes in West Oakland, and they looked exactly as they did in the '90s.

Oakland's skyline was just as I left it. Perfect. San Francisco's buildings got taller, though. I expected that. San Francisco was a city meant to sit at eye level with the sky because its head always seemed to be in the clouds. Some things don't change, even if skylines do. The strange nauseous feeling I used to get as a kid when crossing this bridge wasn't there anymore. I loved this weirdly constructed bridge now. The thing looked like it could collapse on you at any moment, but if that happened, at least I'd die a free man.

But the bridge didn't collapse. We made it to the El Cerrito Del Norte station, and I got off the bus. BART used to be disgusting. It was still dirty, but in the '90s, many BART stations were filled with beggars and hustlers, even in the nice areas. To my surprise, the station was empty. I was greeted by the stench of piss and nobody at all. I looked at the schedule, and I noticed it had been expanded. The trains went to Antioch in the East Bay and San Jose's furthest edges to the south. It didn't matter; I just wanted to get back to Oakland. I asked the station agent how to use the blue card, and, like the bus, I tapped my card on the scanner, and the little reddish-orange barriers shaped like shark fins opened up.

The trains were just as loud as they were in the '90s, maybe even louder. Eventually, my train came, and I got on. I wanted to visit a library in West Oakland. I never read recreationally when I was a young man, but the universe is about balance, as I've learned. When I was young, I felt like I could do anything. The secret in youth's allure is energy, and its Achilles heel is inexperience. To be a God, as Man can understand it, you must be someone with a youthful body, but a mind guided by a soul that has lived many times and found that there isn't glamor in the well-promoted mistakes of the mislead... Or so I would assume.

I discovered the joy of the written word inside of prison. Books filled holes inside of my heart that television couldn't dream of reaching. Spots that I didn't even know were there. Every book is a film if you have the inclination to be a director. And during my time behind bars, I was nothing short of prolific. If stacked flatly on top of each other, the pages I turned and would exceed the height of the highest guard tower in the world. They'd be looking for me on the yard, but their well-trained riflemen could never find me. I was already above them. I was reaching for the sky, the stars, the universe. I was the scientist who crunched the numbers, the astronaut in the suit, and books were the spaceship built for beyond. I was NASA, and they were just an employee of the California Department of Corrections. He may have gotten to leave the prison every day, but he'd never left the planet...

The train was relatively empty. Just me and a few drunks who had nowhere else to be. We stopped at MacArthur, and a few more people, respectable types, got on. They had thin laptops and form-fitting jeans. They looked like they had to go to San Francisco to do something meaningful. Or maybe they were like me, ex-cons on their way to a library. There was no way of knowing. The judgmental among us are the unreliable narrators of life. Everyone had a story, and you can't critique a book you haven't read.

The tunnels screeched just like they did when I was a young man, and then I heard it: "WEST OAKLAND, WEST OAKLAND STATION. THIS IS THE LAST OAKLAND STOP.

NEXT STOP: EMBARCADERO. THIS IS AN SFO-MILLBRAE BOUND TRAIN."

I took a deep breath and got off the train. The feeling was beautiful. I used my little blue card again to exit the station. Things were the same, yet very different. West Oakland was historically Black Oakland, and there was still plenty of Black folk around, but there were other types of people, too; the types I encountered on the train — the slender laptop crowd, they were here now. And kids with pink hair and tattoos. But not like the tattoos in San Quentin. These were different. I saw a slender white girl who was bald, wearing black boots, shorts, and a tank top. She had the word "FUCK" on her forearm in capitalized block letters. These types have always found a way for themselves in San Francisco, but they were historically more cautious in Oakland, things change. I wasn't bitter.

Speaking of change, the Acorn Projects looked fancy. They looked like those condominiums you'd see people with good jobs live in on TV. I was somewhat nervous to walk past them, but the new look helped quell my anxiety. These were low rise and designed to appear unthreatening. I couldn't tell you if the new sanitized look was justified, I hadn't walked past these since the early '90s, but it was hard to envision crack being sold in a place that I could also see Martha Stewart living in. I walked past the apartments without incident. Oakland had gotten calmer, that was for sure. Well, at least on those few blocks. Once I got further down Adeline Street, Oakland started to look like Oakland again. Old Victorian housing blocked from the street by black wrought iron fences, burglar bars on windows worn by rust, and graffiti painted sporadically as far as the eye could see. I was feeling that euphoric feeling. You know, the one brought on by old memories in familiar places? That thing called Nostalgia. Yes, I was nostalgic.

I spotted a man jogging in the distance heading towards me. He was wearing shorts well above his knee, and he had a fanny pack. The fanny pack said "Supreme" on it. I was bewildered by choice of the word "supreme." What was especially odd to me was that someone embroidered it on a fanny pack. The fanny pack jogger man wasn't paying attention and ran right into me. He looked at me with anger in his eyes and said, "Watch where you're fucking goin', man!"

I punched him directly in his mouth. He fell onto his back, and I stomped his head in. I stomped and stomped and stomped again. I broke his teeth, kneeled, and held his nostrils shut with my thumb and index finger. I covered his mouth tightly with the palm of my hand and watched the terror in his eyes as he swallowed his broken teeth... Well, that's what I visualized myself doing, but I controlled my anger, forced a smile, and said, "My bad, man."

He jogged by without responding. I'm glad I held back. Who knows? He may have whipped my ass and made me swallow my teeth. To be completely honest, that was the most aggressively I've seen someone in a fanny pack behave in my life. Maybe he knew something I didn't. Perhaps he knew I wanted to go to a library, not back to a penitentiary.

I walked a few more blocks, and there it was: Oakland Public Library: West Oakland Branch. I entered the building, and it smelled like old books. What a pleasant smell! Only the librarian and I were there. I approached her and pulled out a list of all the books banned in the California State Prison System that I had found interesting. The list was rather extensive. Close to 100 books in total. I handed her the list and said, "I want to read these." She looked up at me and replied, "All of them, why?"

I smiled and answered, "Because I'm free."

They Burn

Have little to lose.

So if you lose everything, it's not much.

Poverty is a gift.

Utilize it.

Would you rather slip off of a curb or jump off the top floor of the

Empire State Building?

California has wildfires. People live near places that burn.

Sometimes their houses burn.

Sometimes they burn.

They burn in their houses, with their things, things they bought.

Oftentimes, they could've left their houses, but they didn't want to leave their things.

Things that burn.

So... They burn...

They burn with their things.

Nostalgia is a Fraud

There's something about the end.

That makes you look fondly

On the past.

With someone.

Shared laughs,

Moments,

Dreams.

But nostalgia is a fraud

And hope is a liar

Truth is
Good things
Don't end
By choice.

Empty

The emptiness of an empty wallet
Isn't as empty
As the emptiness
Of an empty soul.
We can only like so many things.
Our attention span can only
Take so much.
Endless Netflix queues
Robbing us of our ability to pick something
To watch
So, we scroll
And we browse
You can watch anything
The problem with people
Who can
Watch anything
Is a lot like the problem with people
Who can do anything
They end up doing
Nothing.
But they pretend they are
Because who knows?
Someone may be watching.

Backpack Full of DVDs

When I was a kid, I remember I used to buy DVD boxsets of my favorite TV shows.

I would put them in my backpack and take them to school.

When I was bored in class, I'd open my backpack and look at the cover art.

It was usually Family Guy.

Sometimes it'd be Aqua Teen Hunger Force.

Sometimes it was an anime I had found during my many late nights binge-watching Adult Swim.

I would look at the DVDs and knew that there was a break to the monotony.

I knew that eventually it'd be me, my favorite shows and solitude.

As we age, it feels that these small things no longer provide that guarantee.

We still have our backpacks and carrying cases.

But when we look inside of them

There's no reminder of an ideal escape

Just empty space.

Waiting to be filled.

Like Me

Why doesn't writing look like me?

I don't mean racially.

Grow the fuck up.

Every room I've been in

Filled with writers

Felt the same.

Upper middle class attention seekers

Young men in blazers wearing nail polish
And a single earring dangling off of one of their ears
Talking about zines or Amazon's self-publishing program
Poorly explained tattoos that start at the wrist
And work their up the forearm
That seemed to only exist
To make me feel sick
"Is that a tattoo of a typewriter?" I'd ask
"Yeah," they'd answer.
"Cool," I'd reply
I'm loud and goofy
Or withdrawn and quiet
I'm not a goofy person in actuality.
And my mind isn't quiet
I can't quite seem to connect to others
In conversations that can't be concluded with a joke
I'm a class clown that has lost the ability to laugh
Which is strange
Because most writers are comedians
They're just not in on the joke.
I am
But I don't laugh.
Because they're not funny.

Dirty 30

Directly adjacent to where my potential rests its head
Procrastination and self-doubt dwell at the bedside
With a pillow at the ready
Watching my eyelids for movement

indicative of the REM sleep cycle

Waiting for a dream to begin

To suffocate me before it finishes.

13 months to 30.

Just turned into 12

Tick Tock.

Happy Birthday.

LoFi

Long drives, LoFi beats and Japanese Jazz

Cars parked on hilltops

With views of the fog, views of the city

The glimmering lights of prosperity reflected off of your windshield

Coffee in Styrofoam cups: Caffeine mixed with a bit of sugar and a splash of cream

The warm embrace of a hand to hold

The calm of raindrops falling onto the roof of your car

Fog horns blow, sound replacing sight on an unpredictable sea.

We're in an unpredictable place.

Things move forward without forewarning

That's why these seemingly predictable things hold such beauty

Because sitting still on a spinning planet can feel impossible

Until you do...

Barnes and Noble at the El Cerrito Plaza

I like to drive to El Cerrito

I browse the Barnes and Noble and pretend my book is there.

I sit at the coffee shop

I pay third wave prices for first rate garbage

$5.00 for 12 ounces of caffeinated diarrhea, 4 ounces of milk and what must be a pound of sugar to make the shit palatable.

I lift my facemask and take a sip.

I see people taking indirect routes to maintain 6 feet of separation.

I think about crowded buses, trains and foot traffic.

I think about the virus and what it means.

I miss the minor inconveniences of the open world

Traffic sucked, but at least you had somewhere to be.

ESSENTIAL WORKER

I was sitting at my desk. My mind was blank, there's a fog that comes over you after you've been working in an office around the 4th or 5th hour. You basically forget how to do your job. Everything was just muscle memory. My mind was absent, but my fingers remained agile. I don't know why or how this happens, but it does, a lot.

I was taking an application for what is known in financial institutions as a 'disaster loan' or the more consumer-friendly 'hardship loan.' The man on the other end of the phone was crying. He could barely control himself. There was no masculine posturing -- just a man placed on his knees by an unfair system. The economies of The World were shutting down due to a new virus that began in China and spread its tentacles to all four corners of the globe.

I felt bad. This man had just opened his business over the past summer. He was happy with the direction things had been going. He wasn't necessarily making money, but he hadn't lost any either. But then people started getting sick, and some of those sick people started to die and people with money realized they too can die, so the markets crashed and the Governments of The World said, "Everyone stay inside until the rich feel immortal again!"

So, we did. The only people who were allowed out were 'the essential workers.' According to someone I was an essential worker.

Worthless.

Silicon Valley

This new life.

This great leap forward

Has reduced us to nothing more than rhythm and algorithm.

Curated realities keeping us in place

What we see in the future is determined by what we saw in the past.

No more questions

Because we already have our answers

Tailormade

Suited to fit us.

Gated communities of thought hoisted high above the clouds

taking up intangible space

Creating enormous clutter

Delusional minds populating a dying planet

With nothing between them

But empty space

Filled with clutter

Sirens

Sirens whistle under pale moonlight

The sound of slow-moving wind scatters leaves on cracked concrete

Heaven is a stone's throw away from hell

Birds chirp by my window

A mattress is below me

A ceiling is above me

I have a roof over my head
But my heart remains unsheltered
Jumping from place to place
Searching for solutions
It wanders the streets
And I sit in bed, hoping it finds its way home
I don't get sufficient sleep
And I feel my short-term memory fading
I'm always tired
Always fatigued
I think about death
More than I should

Under the Moon

She doesn't click like on my poetry anymore
But I know she reads it.
She doesn't comment on my selfies
But I know she sees them.
She doesn't talk to me as much anymore
But I know she misses me
My stupid voice
Sarcastic quips
Self-deprecating undertones
With a bit of class rage sprinkled on top
Aimed at everything and nothing
At the same time.
I look at the water
And wonder
Like I often do

At the infinite possibilities

And the alternate universes

Where I wasn't such a joke

My procrastination

My second guessing

Anxiety

Absurdity and aloofness

What did I have to show for myself?

The best time of day is when the moon is visible

As the sun is setting

It's at that specific moment where you think you can have it all

The possibilities of daylight

And the comfort of night

But the sun continues to sink behind the western mountain ranges

And the light gives way to impenetrable darkness.

But for a few minutes.

Everything was there. You could see it.

It was yours.

At least in your mind

And there's still a bit of light left

There's a moon for a reason

After all.

I Don't Want You

I don't want fame

I don't want money

And I don't want you.

I want the fog that swells off the surface of the ocean

As the coolness of the earth's blood meets the warmth of illumination

I want silence and predictability.

I don't want traffic jams or smog;

Or wildfire smoke

I want wildlife to comfortable roam around me

I want my cat to sit on my lap

And I want books that don't feel like chores for the pretentious

I want what we were all meant to have

And that's not never-ending happiness.

But a sense of place.

If you can look at the ground

And can't tell the difference between standing **in** it

And running **on** it

Then you'll never have to.

As I Sit

As I sit here, in my rented room

I think about the little I have to go back to.

They have moms and dads

Brothers and sisters with the ability to breathe

They have homes

And they have love in those homes.

Nothing to me is more alienating than that.

The sharpest knife is the one wielded by an experience

You've never had.

A warmth you've never felt

And a longing that won't go away

THE HOUSE ALWAYS WINS

The neighborhood I live in sits on a small incline.

In the morning you can see fog make a silhouette of Mount Diablo on the eastern horizon.

Soon rain will come. And golden-brown hills dried and drenched in the California sun will become a mossy green. The house I live in was built in the '30s.

This house stood when the Mafia made Vegas and bombs fell on Pearl Harbor. This house watched as the Navy built ships and the Japanese flew planes. This house was a home when the Zodiac wrote ciphers and shot teenagers just a mile away. AIDS came and killed. Kurt Cobain caught a bullet that smelled like no spirit at all and Michael Jackson danced until he died. The world cried, but the house remained unmoved...

Napa

Flat roads leading to high peaks

Wineries and wildfires

Gymnastics and generalized anxiety disorders

Fingers wet with saliva pressed against the back of your throat

Gag reflexes, Goatees, some guy in a truck whose sunglasses reflect an orange sky.

In his mouth: a cigar

In his mind: nothing

Acidity melting me away

In this car

On this road

in this hell called heaven

Or maybe we're in paradise?

My morbid curiosity

Trying to find the difference

Between the dumpster and the swimming

There's blood in the chlorine

My eyes are burning.

Why aren't yours?

Simmering

My hatred doesn't manifest in strained vocal cords.

Or long stays in county jails

My hatred is of a sarcastic variety.

I look out into the world from a window

And I see that we're built on a foundation of kindling that we're supposed to call granite

And we take it granted.
But it could all burn so easily.
If just a bit of gasoline were to spill
And a lit cigarette fell from careless fingers
You could watch it rapidly wither.
My hatred doesn't cheer on the spreading of the flames
Nor the susceptibility of its fuel
Because my hatred knows I'll burn with them.
And I laugh
And I write
And I hope.

Edge of Glory

We just met
We're going to have sex
Then you're going to leave
This is the life for me.
Pandemic Tinder and solitude.
Anxieties over STDs and COVID-19
Dead end jobs
Rented rooms
And writing.
Long drives
In beautiful cities
That I can't afford
Gunshots overheard in the ones I can.
I'm from a place that doesn't want me
No matter how bad I want it.
So, I sit on the edge of glory

Like a Lady Gaga song
But no one's singing.
At least not to me.

Fuck

Sitting alone in a room
Is always the best time to examine
The things you do when the room you're in is populated
With people
People who also sit alone in rooms
And feel superior to you
The same way you feel superior to them
When you're protected from the gaze
Of any ego
Other than your own
By four walls built by people
People
People,
You seem to think
You don't need.

Richmond is a City in Syria

I hike in the hills overlooking where skyline views meet the refinery fumes.

Where the bright lights of prosperity's promise blind the discarded at the end of the Bart Line

The whistle of gunfire can't be heard up here.

The canyon promises peace in a place of pride and fleeting purpose.

Richmond, California:

The East Bay borderlands situated between the urban and industrial corridors.

White flight's first suburban victim.

Redlines creating Walnut Creeks for the wealthy to drown in

Rotting away.

Dark orange chemical containment tanks sit beautifully under the gaze of a picturesque mountain.

And I sit on a bench, taking it all in with you.

Quietly perched above despair.

This is the first time I've felt happiness in a while.

I like to make people laugh, but behind the sarcasm and absurdity there Is a sadness I have trouble

articulating.

So, I don't.

ENCAMPMENT

I awoke to bright light and a loud voice.

"The city of San Francisco has designated this an un-lawful encampment. Please vacate the premises immedi-ately," the disembodied voice demanded.

I shivered, as I did every morning, my fingers were stiff as if hardened with rigor mortis, but death hadn't taken me yet. I was very much alive. If I were dead, the police wouldn't require me to stand and collect my belongings in trash bags. Instead, they'd just put me in a body bag, which is a trash bag with some added pretension, before inevitably taking me to a graveyard, a sentimental landfill of sorts.

I had stuffed three pillows, two pairs of pants, an un-counted number of shirts, and a few books in the trash bags in two minutes. The only pair of shoes I owned were already on my feet. Before I departed, a female officer with sad eyes and pale skin handed me a card. It was a tiny tribute to bu-reaucracy. There were numbers for the Department of This & That and a myriad of other organizations; none of the ser-vices appealed to me. Maybe at some point, they would, but the last thing I wanted was to hear the sorrowful voice of a social worker. I was waiting for death or revolution and set-tled on death a long time ago. But, in typical fashion, my body hadn't caught up with my mind.

I began walking. The movement helped to quell my shivers. The blood flow provided natural warmth to my cold exterior. Above my head was a maze of freeway onramps and offramps. I listened to the slow movement of cars, the honking, and the rumbling stereo systems. During rush hour traffic, you can feel the collective aggression reach a boiling point. Something about being trapped in metal, suspended in the air by cement, and reduced to little more than inanimate by a kaleidoscope of faces that sit perpetually in your way does something sinister to the soul. But so does sleeping on concrete, so who was I to judge?

I used to read Philip K Dick when I was younger. His stories predicted all of this. While not every word he wrote came to pass, he accurately described what it would feel like to have the very foundation of what it meant to be human questioned by an ever-evolving, ever-redefining, and ever-expanding force of technological capability. The essence of humanity used to be based on the cognitive ability to reason derived from organic matter. That's what the philosophers taught. Which philosopher? Who fucking cares? A good one. Probably. We don't remember the philosophers. Thinking is how you become homeless. Drugs numbed the thoughts but reduced productivity. You needed to be dumb but productive. That was the ticket. When I felt smart, I didn't want to make the product for philosophical reasons, and when I was high, my body lacked the ability. I was meant to sit in apartments, get high, read books, and talk about the books with people who got high and read books with me. Those people didn't exist, and I read alone. Well, not entirely alone.

There were the others in the encampment. There were always others. Sometimes they talked to you. Other times they spoke to themselves. The homeless cried more than the general population. There was always one weeper. In case you were wondering, a weeper was someone who cried constantly. Every encampment had a weeper, and the weepers usually had tents. New tents. Newly homeless with new tents bought from Target. One of the last things they'd buy was a tent. They'd think about stealing it but would end up buying it, usually with a secured credit card. The bank wouldn't approve them for an unsecured credit line, so they're forced to pay interest on their own money, just to be given the privilege of being in debt.

Can you imagine being so worthless you have to prove you're worthy enough to drown in debt? They max out their $250 secured credit card on a nice tent, and they don't want to be associated with the others. When they first set up, they do so near the encampment, but not quite in it. Usually, a block or so away, but their differential placement inspires differential treatment, and the police push them along. Sometimes the cops even confiscate the tent, and they have to buy another one. That is when the crying starts in earnest. Eventually, someone offers them a drink, and they bonded with whoever offered it to them. Then they talk about their old job or what they aspired to be... "I was in school to be a," they say.

Above me, the horns kept honking. I looked over and made eye contact with 'Odd Todd.' I wasn't sure if his name was actually Todd, but people told me his name was 'Odd Todd' and 'Odd Todd' never objected, so I assumed it to be true. 'Odd Todd' named pigeons and made friends with them. When 'Odd Todd' told me he and the pigeons were comrades in a mutual struggle against the "overbearing hand of the demon-hearted demigods." I didn't believe him, but one day I saw them assist Todd when he was in the middle of a fight with a cop. The cop looked like an action figure from the 1970s. He was tall, blond, and muscular. Odd Todd was on the losing end of the scuffle, but then he whistled, and all of that changed. Within seconds hundreds of pigeons began swarming the action figure cop. They pecked at his face. In less than a minute, blood was leaking from the cop's forehead and dripping into his eyes. Odd Todd kicked the cop in the stomach and was able to get away. Once Todd was too far for the cop to catch up, the pigeons dispersed. Ever since then, I started taking 'Odd Todd' more seriously. He was a man of power in an Alfred Hitchcock kind of way.

Odd Todd approached me and placed his hand on my shoulder. "You know what to do," he said with a smile before going on one of his typical rants.

"The moon shines when the sun dies. Don't you understand? The sun is a symbol of good. You know? But you can't look at it! Don't bite the hand that feeds. That's what they say, but because they're scared. They're fucking scared. There's light in the dark, too. Too much light and the world goes blind. The moon will guide us. As Joseph said, 'he who follows the glow of the moon and rejects the warmth of the sun shall lift us all to prosperity!' You know what to do, Arthur!" I looked at him. He was manic again. There was some genius in his insanity, but most of it was just insanity. I began to walk away, but Todd ran ahead and stopped directly in front of me.

"I don't know what you're talking about, Odd. Can you please just let me find a place to rest? I love you, but I'm fuckin' tired." He grabbed both of my shoulders and lightly shook me.

"You know what to do, my boy. Arthur, you know what to do! King Arthur will reign again. Claim the kingdom and spit in the eyes of the false gods!"

My name wasn't Arthur. He just called me that from time to time. Even if I corrected him, it wouldn't change anything. Actions speak louder than letters on birth certificates anyway. Odd's eyes grew wide and hopeful.

"Arthur, look," he said as he pointed to the freeways above us. "They can bypass you, but they can't bypass us all!" He began laughing hysterically. A flock of pigeons flew above Todd and me and began to circle us. They circled three times before scattering. It was a surreal experience. Todd winked at me before walking away.

There was a rusted red car with both of its windows smashed in. The car had been sitting there for months, but it looked like it had been there for years. It was somewhat of a landmark for me. I never sat inside of it before, but the police were only a few blocks away, and if they saw me sit down on the street, there was a reasonably good chance they'd tell me to move. San Francisco went in cycles with us. We'd find a spot, and we'd be there for a few months, then the cops, social workers, and garbage men would come. One job with three titles. The cops would threaten us. The social workers would offer assistance and glare angrily at the aggressive cops without actually intervening. The garbage men would throw away the excess shit we couldn't carry away ourselves.

It was a game of cat and mouse, and no one ever won anything. Speaking of cats, when I opened the car door, a tiny kitten lept out. There was a pile of cat food in the driver's seat, and several kittens in the backseat cuddling with what I assumed was their mom. I didn't want to disturb them, so I quietly closed the passenger door. For some reason, I felt it was my duty to watch over these cats and protect them, so I did. Maybe I could command an army of cats the same way 'Odd Todd' commanded pigeons. I sat down beside the car and decided that if the police came, so be it. It felt nice being near the animals. I wondered who was feeding them, then Odd's words suddenly came back to me. "They can bypass you, but they can't bypass us all!" THEY CAN BYPASS YOU, BUT THEY CAN'T BYPASS US ALL!" Something about that resonated with me.

I dug into my trash bag and pulled out one of my books. The book was *Ask The Dust*, written by a man named John Fante. He was a struggling writer in Los Angeles who wrote about Arturo Bandini, who was also a struggling writer in Los Angeles. The book was funny. There were moments of melancholy, but he navigated them with a sense of humor. I hoped that one day the darkness inside of me could inspire a smile on someone's face, but I was no writer. I didn't even own a computer, let alone a pen. Well, I may have owned a computer. I had a computer in storage, but I hadn't paid the storage bill except for the initial deposit due upon receiving the key to the unit. I assumed that the storage company auctioned off my stuff. If my belongings were sold,

I wasn't bitter about it. I didn't need much. I just felt genuine sympathy for whoever bought my old computer and various other things so worthless I failed to remember they were.

I began reading but had trouble focusing. I noticed someone walking toward me and recognized them as Meredith. Meredith was a peculiar looking woman. Her hair was silver, and her skin was so orange that if she had told me that before ending up in San Francisco, she had lived on the sun, I certainly wouldn't have believed her, but I'd take a second to consider the possibility.

"Where to next?" asked Meredith.

"I don't know. We are going to be kicked out no matter where we go. It's just a matter of time," I replied. A single pigeon landed on my shoulder, and Odd Todd's words echoed in my brain: "BUT THEY CAN'T BYPASS US ALL!" I leaned my head against the car and ruminated on our situation as the gentle purrs of sleepy cats comforted my ears.

"You know what?" I asked.

"What?"

"We should take over the Bay Bridge."

"What do you mean take over the Bay Bridge?" Meredith asked as her eyes widened.

"I mean, we take our shit and plant our asses right in the middle of the bridge. Block traffic going both ways. Fuck it. Whenever there's a police shooting, they do it in Oakland.

Some moms took over a house in Oakland, and the media made it a big thing, now they're getting to keep the house," I continued, "why can't we do the same shit on the bridge and solve the problem for all of us?"

"The cops will just make us move."

"The cops can't make us move. We allow them to move us."

"Since when did you get so fuckin' tough, huh? I didn't see you putting up much of a fight when they woke you up and told you to kick rocks."

"You have to pick your battles," I said with a shrug.

"Well, I ain't camping on the fuckin' bridge."

"Who's forcing you? But what do you have to lose?"

"My life."

"What life?"

"Fuck you," she replied. Her eyes wandered, and she stared at the kittens in the car. "So, you're the one feeding these cats?"

"Nope. Just watching over them.

"Why?"

"Because when things are bad, there's something inside of me that wants to protect the few good things left. Plus, they're adorable." Meredith sat beside me and leaned her head on my shoulder.

"Tell me something wonderful."

"There are cats in the car, and they will never know how dumb this all is."

"How do you know they don't know? They might know."

"Good point. I never asked the cats. I'll be sure to ask in the future."

"Shut up," she replied with a quiet laugh. Then we just sat there. Her head sat still on my shoulder next to the rusted car filled with kittens. I closed my eyes, and the pigeon flew away...

Christmas in Vallejo

Christmas lights fastened to chain link fences

Dogs bark at passing cars

Santa is coming to town

America's consumerist obsession manifest

As a morbidly obese man

Carrying bags filled with new products for the prosperous

And new debt for the impoverished

Rain, fog and snow

Batter tents along the roads

In the alleys

And under the overpasses

But Santa never seems to notice them

When he passes over

He's never in town long enough to look.

Aesthetics

Dressed for a war that won't come.

The counter cultures act a lot like the cultures they think they're countering.

Puritans with plastic morals, social media hashtags and hair dyes.

Were the '60s like this?

Was there truth in the romance?

Or was it just a different generation of rich kids

Pretending to be activists.

The Vietnam war was still fought.

The kids came from somewhere.

The colleges screamed for change.

They marched in Berkeley.

But they never had to pick up the guns

The kids who couldn't get into Berkeley did.

Labor exploitation is old

It's been done.

And it's still being done

But that's not enough

The offspring of the factory owners

Need to augment their morality with advocacy

Your life matters.

Of course it does!

Who else is going to work for free?

Yas queen.

Slay.

Wrong Side of the Right Water

The northeastern shores.

Where the bays of San Francisco and San Pablo meet
the Carquinez Strait and the Delta.

Where the industries of the past are the polluters of the present.

Where the word affordable is based on relativity

Where warehouse workers are punished because they were
born to close

to where people make a starting pay of 80k a year to give
PowerPoint presentations with grammatical errors that include words like "synergy" and terms like "public-private
partnerships"

I'm smart to make the presentations, but too lazy to get the paperwork to prove it

I'm strong enough to lift the boxes in the warehouses, but it'd hurt too much to think my body only existed to move pallets of frozen food around for the profit of people who don't care about me.

The black ones live in Richmond and Vallejo

The brown ones live in San Pablo

And white ones perpetually feigning superiority live in Crockett, Martinez and Rodeo

But we're all here.

And we're all poor

Credit Score

After your morning cup of coffee

Remember to check your credit score

After checking your credit score

Remember to check those real estate websites

Zillow, Trulia, Redfin and the rest

Look at the things you can't afford

Look at the mansions

Look at the trees

Look at the hills that these mansions sit on

Surrounded by the trees

Trees that grow naturally

Trees that don't seem to grow

Near you

Air fresh off the ocean

Pictures of

Oil tankers

Taken from windows

Taken by widows

Taken properly

Taken to sell property

Property with a view

Of a vast ocean

Meant to attract people

Just not to people like you

You're more the type to wait for these vessels of economics

Delivering oil to be refined

So, your gas tank can be refilled

There's cherry trees and orange trees in the backyard of the garden

Of one of the homes

There's also a small bench with partial views of the pacific

You'd read there.

With a warm cup of coffee in your hand

And you'd look at the ocean

And it'd be so beautiful that you might cry

Not in front of others

Just to yourself

Like always

Alone

Achievement porn:

A dangling carrot of prosperity

Presented in such great detail

That you forget

You're on the wrong side of the computer screen.

Speakers, Listeners, and Outliers

There are three types of people in this world:

Speakers, listeners and outliers.

The speakers speak

The listeners listen

And the outliers simply... exist.

There's no such thing as thought as most people don't think.

They repeat.

The conflicts of the world can be categorized by the ideology of the outliers

The presentation of the speakers

And the empty minds of the listeners

Death for symbolism

Systems built by words without definition

To be taught by interpreters whose interpretations are debated in perpetuity

Law is an argument in suits using words you don't quite recall in English class

By men whose leadership you never asked for

Yet they're always asking you

To do

And you will do

Or you won't

And if you don't

You will be pushed aside

Because in the presence of power

The only true curse word is...

Why?

Arnold Industrial

Arnold Industrial Way,

North Concord,

Contra Costa County,

California

In a warehouse

On bunk beds

Home to

The surplus people

This is where they sleep

Their hair

Home to lice

Their skin

Home to scabies

But nowhere is home to them

America doesn't have a government

America has a human resources department

And these people

Have been

Let go.

REFRIGERATOR

I woke up in the middle of the night. I wanted to go back to sleep, but I just had to check my phone and now, three hours later, I'm wide awake, writing this. I went to the kitchen and stood there in the dark. I opened the refrigerator, not out of hunger, but habit and then I closed it and the room was dark again. I stood there in the dark for a few minutes. I was motionless. I thought about the options I have. I thought about leaving in the middle of the night, deleting my ever-expanding social media footprint and working as a delivery driver or something stupid and easy.

I sat down on the kitchen floor. I opened the refrigerator again, placed my head inside of it and allowed my cheek to touch the cold interior. The refrigerator door slowly began to close and tapped my shoulder as my eyes adjusted to the brightness inside. I turned my head and stared at the bag of romaine lettuce beside me. It instructed me to wash the lettuce before eating it. I felt the urge to throw away all of the food and remove the cabinets to make room for my entire body. Even if i removed all of its contents, my body is too big to fit and even if it did, how the fuck would I explain that to my roommates?

"Why did you take everything out of the fridge and get in," they'd ask. I'd probably say "I don't know," and offer to replace any food that may have spoiled. I stood up and closed the refrigerator door. It was dark.

I thought of New York City, Paris, Rome and Tokyo. I thought of all those places and all of the lights. Millions of heads at eye level with the warning labels on romaine lettuce inside of open refrigerators. I started laughing. I needed a bigger fridge and more lettuce.

I also enjoy tomatoes.

What If I Can't Write Anymore?

What if the words don't come
Like I've counted on them to
What if I'm cursed.
Cursed to be the man of nil
Cursed to almost be
But never actually become
What if the apple doesn't fall
What if the apple didn't fall far
What if the apple is rotten
And the tree is dead, withering
What if the light in my eyes isn't my own
Only a reflection of someone else
What if I'm wrong about the good
And what if I'm right about the bad
What if this is all for nothing
And the sad shit I say isn't unique
And the happy shit I say is a lie
What if I'm constantly misunderstood
What if they get sick of me
What if Hell is real and God is mad at me
What if this is hell?
What if this is heaven and I'm fucking dumb
What if this is a hell of my own making
What if I'll never be more than a memelord
What if I die
I will die
But what if
The minute it happens

I wanted to live
What if I'm reincarnated
What if that reincarnation has everything
Everything I ever wanted in this life
What if it doesn't matter
What if i can't *RIGHT* anymore?
What if I'm wrong.

It's Not That Complex

The world isn't that hard to understand.
There are people with things.
They want to keep those things.
They'll lie to you.
And if you have the courage to confront them
The people who don't will kill you.
That's the history of the world.
You don't need the names
The names and the nations don't matter.
History is just an echo chamber of egos.
If you can't be the one written about
At least you can be the one writing about it.
If you're any good
They might write about you
But they probably won't.
And you'll just have to live with that

Attorneys & Firearms

Attorneys and firearms serve the same purposes but for different types of people.

Problem solvers.

Devices and disciplines that make the things we dislike disappear

The educated will bury you in paperwork and words rooted in Latin

The others will burrow bullets deep into your skin until you're buried under the dirt

Dirt that will feed on you as you decompose

The same dirt that supports and sustains the trees.

The same trees that will be logged and turned into paper

Paper that words will be written on

Words that will be used to bury you.

In debt and arguments over interpretation of fluid definitions

Humanity

Divided by the level of effort and sophistication behind our brutality

Veneers of civility is the only thing that keeps a civilization going.

The moment that nihilism has a greater influence than tradition on what governs

Is the day your world dies

It's the circle of life

And it wouldn't be life without death

Right?

Feelz

There's an alternate universe that I visit on occasion.

Where you and I awake in the same bed

Under the same roof

And share in the same dream.

I make you coffee to combat your grogginess

And I feel your lips press against mine

And in the moment

I'm not jealous of anyone anymore

My insecurities get carried away

by the waters that ebb and flow on this particular edge of
the earth

And I feel okay.

Indecision has a way of making decisions.

And in this alternate universe

Indecision died

The moment we decided on each other.

WHAT A WASTE

"You ever feel like you've wasted your life?" That's what I said to my best friend on the phone as I walked to my car. I just left Best Buy where I was looking for one of those stupid iPhone dongles because Apple's unquenchable need for perpetual growth made them get rid of the auxiliary port and forced this overpriced proprietary USB variant down the consumer's throat. I wanted to listen to DaBaby in my car with the curse words uncensored, so there I was, in Best Buy, doing exactly what Apple wanted me to do, consuming.

"Um. It depends on the day. Have you taken your sad bitch pills today, Abe" I hadn't, but that wasn't the point. I was disturbed by something in Best Buy. More accurately, I was disturbed by Best Buy's lack of something. CDs. The CD section was utterly gone. There was not a single compact disc for sale in the entire store. The iPhone dongle was sold out, so I decided I'd buy it from Amazon. I fucking hated Amazon, but I hated walking into stores and asking employees with dead eyes where iPhone dongles were even more. Either way, I was supporting capitalism. Cancer is cancer; the aggressiveness of cancer doesn't change the fact that the body will eventually die. Best Buy was a less profitable business than Amazon. Cancer is cancer.

I used to take the bus to Best Buy from my apartment in Downtown Martinez to buy CDs. Some days I'd take the County Connection bus to Pleasant Hill. Other days I'd take the WestCat to Pinole. It made the journey less mundane. The bus ride to Pleasant Hill was 10 minutes less than the bus ride to Pinole, but I found the Pinole ride to be more enjoyable. I liked the rolling hills of Cummings Skyway and the bay views that accompanied them. It was one of the things in my turbulent childhood that I looked fondly upon. And just like that, without a single bit of consideration for how I might feel, they were gone. Brick and mortar stores decided CDs were no more. Spotify, Apple, Amazon, and the internet replaced them. I thought about how quickly our lives flashed before our eyes. How the things we loved that filled our days with joy became antiquated. And antiquity is only celebrated when coupled with profitability. I wanted to buy a CD, play it in my car. I'd probably never listen to it afterward, but I just wanted to hold one. I wanted to read the liner notes; look at the photos in the booklet. There was something cathartic about that. It felt like you were truly getting to know the artist. A good CD booklet could remove the levels of separation between you and the people who created the music you loved.

I wasn't a child anymore. Life was taking its toll on me. My dreams about becoming a celebrated writer, someone of literary merit, felt further away than usual at that moment. Vanishing youth has a way of reminding you of your failures. Society moves on; whether you sink or swim, it moves on, and you have to swallow it, and it, whatever it is, always tasted like piss to me. Life was about how long you could smile with someone else's piss filling your mouth. You had to smile, you had to fake appreciation, or you would eventually be cut off and die of thirst.

I was nearing 30, and I had no idea of whether or not the thing that I was working toward would bear fruit. Was I wasting my life? I hadn't the faintest clue, but one thing was for sure: Best Buy wasn't selling CDs anymore. And nobody gave a fuck. I got in my car, told my friend I had to go, turned on the radio and pretended to enjoy it.

One more gulp of piss wouldn't kill me.

Nothing to Burn

Crimson orange dominated the sky
And complaints filled my mind
As ash covered my windshield
Obscuring the road in front of me.
I took a deep breath
I smelled the smoke
I breathed in your home
Your equity
Your American dream filled my lungs
And I coughed.
I still wanted it, though.
I checked my accounts.
Nothing to burn yet.
Nothing at all.

Uninspired

An oil tanker leaks toxins into the Pacific
while a honey bee
Hundreds of miles away
pollinates a flower
A bomb goes off
at precisely
the same time
as a baby is born.
A man finds a winning lottery ticket in a trashcan
while searching for something to eat
A gay celebrity secretly eats a Chick Fil A Chicken Sandwich

A straight pastor secretly sucks a dick
Both enjoyed it more than they expected
They won't admit they did it, though
It'd be bad for business
A white mom posts a picture of Martin Luther King
With an out of context quote on social media
While watching Michelle Obama's speech during the DNC
To atone for calling the cops on a black teenager
Power walking in her neighborhood
It made her nervous
Better safe than sorry...

A Longer Version of That Popular Nike Ad

Don't let the book close on you.
Shoot your shot
If you miss,
You miss
But let the gunpowder residue coat your fingers
You'll look back on it
I promise,
You will.
You'll find a memory to smile upon
Even if you fail
You'll be able to reminisce
About what it was like
To feel the warmth of hope's arms
Gently embracing you.
It's okay to die
But it's not okay

Not to live
You don't owe them
And they don't own you.
Don't let the long hours,
Pained sighs,
And weary eyes of the crowd
Put out the fire burning within
It's the only thing keeping you
From burning alive

The Low Prices of a Pandemic

There's no prison
No warzone
No funeral
That is quite as depressing as a Wal-Mart during a pandemic.
People standing in lines
Weary of everyone
Carts overflowing with things made in bulk
Dark circles under tired eyes
Accentuated by the glare
Of fluorescent lighting
a middle aged security guard
Always
With a holstered firearm
Who dreamt of being a cop
Standing next to a yellow bench with a statue of Ronald McDonald
Protecting the richest family in the world

From the poorest

A failure policing those never allowed to fail

Everyday we casually observed

Passive atrocity

But this one is different

We're all vulnerable

We can't pretend it's not real

And what do we do?

We go to Wal-Mart

To stock up on toilet paper

Because

We're all full of shit.

NO ONE DIES HARDER

No one dies harder than a writer. Each and every one of us has a rendezvous with death, but writers have a relationship with it. They get to know its face, its body language, and other little that one could only notice after a comradeship had formed. You even begin to notice when death's gained some weight or when he did laundry and the black cloak smells of the roses left by the bereaved.

Bereavement: basically, a term for the victims of death that haven't died. I've never seen death, well, I've seen dead bodies, but I've never seen death, like the dude, but I know he hangs around me. My heart skips beats every now and then and I know death is just playfully reminding me I'm his world.

I've decided Death is a man. And he's always per-plexed. He's confused. He can't wrap his head around how he could be so popular, yet so ignored? If Time Magazine were an honest publication, Death would be crowned "Person of the Year" every year. The only reason we honestly have a person of the year is because of him. Time Magazine wouldn't even have a fucking name for its publication it if weren't for Death's Midas touch. Time exists because death told us it will run out, so we have cyclical lists, and we count the cycles until we have to kick it with Death, who is defi-nitely a dude.

It's cold in my room. The home I live in was built in the '30s and has poor insulation and the temperatures are dropping quickly around the Bay Area. I'm struggling with writer's block. I'm only writing to district myself from the depression. I'm not inspired. I thought about how heartbreaking life can be and how death may be a relief, if not at least a release. I started to think about death as not an enemy, but an indifferent ally to the aching among us. I'm aching, but I'm also afraid.

No one dies harder than a writer. That's why we're friends.

Dog In the Race

Stop whispering.
Just say it aloud.
You're allowed
To have thoughts
You're allowed to murder...
The image
Someone else created for you
If the mold they cast for you
Is killing...
You
It's okay to kill...
It.
Are you okay with that?
It doesn't matter.
Pick a side
Have a dog in the race
Pick yourself
No one else will

Solitude's Contradiction

I find myself in a conundrum of sorts.
I crave solitude
I crave it to such an extent
That the presence of others
Often feels painful
But being alone creates its own set of burdens
At night,

In the dark

In the moments closest to what I have grown to crave.

A type of sadness envelops me.

A new sort of restlessness

A sleepless ache

Discovers my secrets

Whispers into my ear

And reminds me

That the restlessness

Doesn't originate from the people i so desperately flee

It comes from within

And that no amount of solitude

Shuttered blinds

Or Shut-off lamps

Will ever be sufficient enough

To hide me

From what I truly want to escape.

Myself.

Social anxiety.

You're a deer in headlights

You're used to having it all figured out.

You're seamless in your mind.

Flawless in your delivery.

But your fantasy

And its expectations

Have been divorced from the reality

The one you're living in

For a long time

When was the last time you looked in someone's eyes, felt a
spark

Allowed the flame to grow

Without your hesitation, constant need for noise

So useless that even you

Hate the words

Falling from your lips

Like suicide jumpers

Set ablaze by jet fuel

Lungs filled with smoke

Falling from the world trade center

To be splattered on the empire state's

Imperial streets

Stop talking.

Feel the wind.

Take a breath

It's okay.

You don't have to be on all the time

Sometimes

It turns people off.

Fuck It

The insincere
Will always exist.
That's not your problem.
Your problem is you.
The storms will come.
The sun will shine
The leaves will fall

So will you
But you choose whether you tumble
From your
FEET
Or on your
Knees

I Like You a Lot, Okay?

I've never really seen them,
But
I can't unsee them:
Your
E y E s
It's crazy
2 me
That a world
Established
by genocide
Could EVER
Produce something as soothing as your eyes
But maybe that's what causes the
Death
Destruction
and
Deterioration
Because we'd never allow
Something so beautiful
2 b had without
A fight.

THE SAME OLD NEW BEGINNING

When you start a new job, you get that jolt of excitement. You feel like an explorer of uncharted economic opportunity. You think to yourself, hope to yourself, that this one will be different. These 40-hour weeks will melt away fast like a stick of butter over an open flame.

It will be enjoyable. If you love what you do you never have to work a day in your life. But by day three or maybe day four, that excitement slowly begins to wane. The ones forced to stand will begin to feel the blisters grow at exactly the same pace as their boss' bluster becomes burdensome. The ones forced to sit will lose sensation in their lower extremities and will be greeted by pins and needles as blood rushes through their idle legs. By the first month your illusion of mobility begins to fade away and you look at your alarm clock like an oppressor.

You may throw it against the wall, but that won't change the regimented way you live in order to qualify for the debt they force you into. Give yourself some credit. You deserve it.

You've been prequalified.

David Foster Wallace Killed Himself

Stop writing to sound smart.

No one really cares about how many words you know.

Extensive vocabularies utilized for the explanation of simple things is superfluous

Look!

I just used the word superfluous

You don't fucking care

Neither do I

See?

Large vocabularies wasted on simple details

Are a bandage

For the gaping wounds

Caused by having nothing to say

You're not David Foster Wallace

And,

Honestly...

You don't want to be.

A description of a chair doesn't need two pages

And your story doesn't need 2,000.

If you can make someone feel a full spectrum of emotions in 5 minutes with words

You have a better understanding of language than the winner of a spelling bee.

Stop writing like you're trying to win a spelling bee

Write like it hurts not to.

There's Something

There's something about the human female.

Something that is

Powerful

More powerful

Than

The most destructive armies

More important

Than the most

Brilliant

Discoveries

We can build all kinds

Of shit.

And the planet knows we can

Destroy

Because we have

But like MOTHER earth

Women can heal.

This is the essence of their gift.

They bring life.

I've seen it.

I've sat alone.

I've punched holes in walls.

Written suicide notes

That remain unpublished

Not due to a love of life

But uncertainty

And ultimately

Cowardice

I've cried alone.

Lived alone.

Felt...

Alone

With others

But sometimes,

When you're alone

One will see you

The right one

And like mother earth

They'll take your dirt

And create a forest

A forest so beautiful

That you'll almost forget about father time who assures you

This won't last.

And you hope he's wrong

Fuel

Don't numb the pain.

Use it.

It's a fuel if you have the right kind of fire.

Most don't have what it takes to turn their tears to gold

But if you do.

They'll glisten brilliantly under the light

Whenever you so choose to step out from under the shadows.

Don't raise children.

Raise yourself up high enough to stand on your own two feet.

There are too many people

They're all in pain

Your ego must be enormous and your intentions cruel to force a human to endure this planet.

Be kind to everyone

Be nice to no one

It's okay to misread maps

They were written by men with no sense of direction.

Relationship Without a Purpose

People without purpose
The purposeless people
Will attempt to fill the void
By latching onto you.
They need admiration
They need the kind words
Everyone likes a compliment now and then
But these people sacrifice their soul
Just for some views and a few likes
Maybe I don't get it.
Attention has come easily to me
In almost anything I've attempted
So maybe I don't understand the value
To those without.
But those without
Are about to be
Without me.

LEAST EDUCATED ON THE ELEVATOR

High-rise residential buildings are a symbol of urban America. If you live in one, you're either at the bottom or the top. My situation puts me closer to the bottom, and the building I was approaching was reserved for those at the top. I was there to pick up a free couch. I pulled up, saw the dark blue reflective glass and a homeless woman sitting on a dirty blanket step from the entrance, and I knew I had reached my destination before the GPS announced that I had arrived. I turned on my hazard lights because street parking in San Francisco was more myth than reality, especially near the high rises. The bustling corners of a city poised on the edge are places where parking is paid for, and I decidedly wasn't paying for a thing. Especially when the money generated would likely go to a tech company as a tax subsidy once the pandemic ended to ensure San Francisco wasn't left in the dust for Austin, Texas, or some other place where artists made something significant happen 20 years ago. I wonder if they would have created anything if they knew that their inspiration and hard work would be used to lure the type of people in that would likely result in nothing of significance happening ever again.

I got out of the rented moving truck and looked around. It was a characteristically windy San Francisco day, and the air from the Pacific felt nice on my skin. I called the number to let the man in the high-rise know I was there to pick up the couch. He picked up after three rings, and his voice was friendly and pleasant. I could tell life had been kind to him. His parents were probably alive and still together. He went to a good college, not his first choice, but his second or third, and he wasn't initially happy, but once he started school, he quickly made friends, and those friends all graduated, and they moved to coastal cities. They would playfully argue about which one was superior. I bet his exgirlfriend, who he was still friends with, probably moved to Los Angeles. LA has captured the mind of the world as quintessentially Californian. It was equal parts ocean and sun. His artist friend who wanted to paint and was a proponent of winter fashion went to Seattle. And this guy, the generous, politically minded couch giving self-identified democratic-socialist that he was, moved to San Francisco. That's the kind of voice he had. His name was Scott.

After a few minutes of staring at myself in the blue reflective glass, I saw him. He looked like his voice, too, clean and proper. He had red hair and was wearing a Stone Temple Pilots teeshirt. I was familiar with the Stone Temple Pilots, but I couldn't name a single song. We did the pandemic handshake, an elbow bump. I don't know who decided this, but everyone started doing it. Maybe it will be one of the things that will outlast the pandemic. His elbow was small and wrapped in freckle-covered sun-sensitive skin. We made small talk as we walked to the elevator to grab the couch. I started to feel uneasy. I felt like I wasn't good enough to be there. Everything and everyone looked put together. Everyone we passed looked like they knew how to do the math problems that I didn't, spoke at least two languages, and had been to Europe or Asia or something. I was likely the tallest person in the building and yet, felt the smallest.

We waited silently for the elevator doors to open. As it arrived and the doors opened, I found the interior of the elevator aesthetically pleasing. It was dimly lit; the walls of the elevator were reflective and connected to dark gold railings. The elevator's ceiling featured a forest painting in the fall, and decorative brown leaves were hanging by threads so thin they were rendered invisible.

"Whoever did the interior designing for this elevator didn't think it all the way through."

He looked at me, eyebrows raised slightly, and he appeared genuinely curious as to what I meant. "The last thing I want to think about in a high-rise elevator is the word fall," I said in a dry tone of voice. He started genuinely laughing, a bit harder than I deemed necessary for a joke I didn't think was that funny. It was just an attempt to fill the silence shared by strangers in a well-decorated elevator that was moving entirely too slowly. Eventually, we made it to his floor. The first thing I noticed as we walked out of the elevator was the carpet in the hallway. It was eerily close to the color and pattern of the carpet in the Vegas shooter's hotel room back in 2017. It made me feel like every property developer went to the same guy for carpets and all that guy had available was the same pattern that hosted chunks of Stephen Paddock's dislodged skull and brain matter. Other than that, the hallway was unremarkable.

"Sorry for the mess. I just moved into this apartment from the second floor," the Generous Ginger remarked as he opened the door to his unit.

"Why'd you move up twenty floors in the same building?" I asked.

As we walked in, he pointed to the unit's large windows with panoramic views of San Francisco and replied, "That's why," with an audible smile in his voice.

The view was beautiful. My eyes were instantly drawn to Sutro Tower. A white cloud with a gray outline was floating between its three prongs, giving the appearance of an elaborate crown, fitting for an imperial city's highest point. We both stood quietly for a few moments to take it in. There were two couches in the apartment, both of which were in good condition.

"So, which couch am I taking?" I asked.

He pointed to an expensive-looking couch that was much nicer in person than it appeared in his online posting and said, "that one."

"Thank you," I said.

"No problem."

"It's a really nice couch."

"Thank you," he responded genuinely, "I know I could have sold it, but I needed it out quickly, and you're using it to furnish your new place, right?"

"Yeah, just moved to a new spot in Oakland."

"That's why I'm giving it to you. A lot of people pick up free furniture just to resell it."

"One man's generosity is another man's side hustle." My indifference at the prospect of someone taking advantage of his kindness seemed to bother him. After a prolonged pause, I asked, "so, do you want to get started?"

We didn't speak as we moved the couch into the hallway. We didn't even make eye contact. We just walked to the elevator. As we waited, I thought of saying something but chose not to. If I made a joke and he didn't laugh, the awkwardness would grow in intensity. I was already out of my element. I didn't belong in this building, standing next to this man. I should have acted shocked at the idea of someone reselling his furniture. He would have appreciated that, and then he could have used the time it took to walk the couch over to the well-decorated elevator to tell me about himself. He would have told me about all the things I suspected about his life but couldn't confirm. I would have listened and nodded, attempting to camouflage myself in the conversation. I'm sure he would have mistaken my agreeableness for relatability. The lies I would have told him about my life would mirror the truths of his. I knew how to play the role, but since we stood in silence, there was no need to.

As we made our way down, the elevator stopped at the 19th floor. The doors opened.

"Hey buddy!" shouted Scott excitedly.

"What's up, Scott?" Replied the man on the 19th floor as he entered the elevator.

"Just getting rid of my old couch." Scott looked toward me and said, "This is Allen. He and I went to Stanford together."

"Nice to meet you, Allen," I replied with a nod. "Allen and I were in Treehacks together," he continued, "we'd party and code all night."

"Then we got jobs and became boring," Allen commented with palpable nostalgia.

Scott chuckled, which seemed to brighten Allen's mood. He was back to being affable. They both appeared pleased with this chance encounter. I wasn't mad at them. I wasn't even envious. Envy is an emotion that implies the presence of a chance. I never felt I had one.

"Where did you go to school?" Asked Scott.

"I'm finishing up my English degree," I answered. "I currently work at a call center as a bank teller and do some tech support on the side." My eyes were glued to the floor. I wanted to lie, but I didn't have it in me.

"Oh, that's cool," Allen replied.

I shrugged. It wasn't cool, not really. There was nothing cool about working a dead-end job. I understood that no response from Allen would be both honest and polite, so he forewent honesty in pursuit of civility. God bless the urbane among us in our urban centers. The burden of tolerance will forever be the crick in their collective necks, but it's at least it's not a noose. Not yet, at least. Give it time. But patience is a virtue that only favors those with time to waste. Time is money, and this building was filled with the patient.

We reached the bottom floor. Scott and Allen shared their goodbyes and planned to meet at Ocean Beach to play frisbee. I maneuvered the couch out of the elevator. Allen gave me the pandemic elbow bump. I didn't understand why he insisted on doing this, especially since I was awkwardly holding a couch. Was he trying to make me feel included? Scott grabbed the other end, and we began to head out to the street.

"Allen and I used to get into all kinds of crazy stuff."

"I'm sure they're still talking about all the wild nights of frisbee and debauchery at Stanford to this day." He knew I was making fun of him. He forced a chuckle. We didn't speak on the second trip up to his apartment for the couch cushions. We grabbed the remaining pieces and headed back down with minimal conversation.

"Well, hope you enjoy the couch," he said in a muted tone. I began to feel like a dick, but then I looked at the gleaming skyscraper where he resided, and the homeless woman with her back leaned against it and knew that a bit of sarcasm was the least I could do.

It was all I could do.

Adulthood

You never really move out of your parents' house.

At a certain age you're just put up for adoption.

Your parents do everything they can to make you the wor-thiest foster child you can be.

Hopefully a good company adopts you.

Hopefully you prove your worth.

If you don't, you become a ward of the state.

The unadopted.

The unworthy

Wayward children find concrete beds on sidewalks

In cells

Wherever they go, they're greeted with concrete

Until there's nothing left.

One's child

No longer

Journalism

Those dead bodies that you hear about

had the ability to hear about you, too.

If you were a disembodied red dot denoting a homicide

on one of these crime tracking maps

On some newspaper's website

that desperately pleads for you to disable your popup blocker

Because reporting now relies on ad revenue

"MALE, AGE 36, SHOT, 1600 BLK MACARTHUR BLVD, OAKLAND"

His 36 years weren't in vain.

He may have sold someone auto insurance.
Or a new mattress.
And at the very least
Provided the extra clicks needed
To carry journalism to the next coffin
Brought to you by State Farm...
"WHAT'S IN YOUR WALLET?"
Wait, wrong company.
Who died?

Good

I'm not a good person.
I'm not sure if I'm a bad person
But.
I assure you...
I'm not a good one, either.
I am scared of everything and everyone.
Even if I know that their intentions are pure.
I second guess them.
I second guess myself into my own personal hell.
Where I am assembling my own personal army.
To defend against the possibility of an enemy.
That is actually a friend
I sit there
Ready for an imagined war.
When the real threat
Is from within.

The Ocean Is Free

Money costs time
But the ocean is free
Every mile inland
Feels like an eternity
I don't want to be trapped in an office
Suspended to land
No sign of buoyancy
I'd rather be trapped
by a dynamic sea
No more land
No more static
Just let the Pacific
Wash over me

I Still Try

If birthed from the womb of an illiterate
Every written word is a revolt within itself.
Fate doesn't exist.
Walls crumble.
Bureaucracies fall
People die
Paperwork gets misplaced
Lives rot away in filing cabinets that can appear taller than skyscrapers
Filled with the names of people that feel smaller than ants.
And despite all of that.
I still try.
You should, too.

LETTER OF THE LAW

When you hear about a crime, what do you think to yourself? Do you think about the individual who committed the crime? Do you think about the victim of the crime? Where does your mind naturally lead you to? Do you come up with a conclusion about the thought processes that led to the criminal act? Is the criminal act actually criminal?

What I mean by that is does it break the *spirit* of the law or does it break the **letter** of the law? And what are the differences between the two? If a child is murdered, we know innately that it is wrong. That is something that should never be allowed to stand in any society; "civilized" or not. Humanity shouldn't tolerate such atrocious behavior. This breaks the spirit of law. There is something inside of you that screams for justice.

Smoking weed and drinking a 40 oz. beer while sitting on the stairs in the middle of an apartment complex is breaking the letter of the law. The letter of the law is worthless. The letter of the law is conditioning. The letter of the law isn't about morality, it's about control. Anything that constricts human behavior when it is victimless isn't about anything but control.

Never let letters legislate your spirit away.

Save your outrage.

Kill your masters.

City Limits

I have a need for a nostalgia that'll never come to pass.

You can't longingly look back on a history that hasn't happened.

Not to you at least.

Pride is something that is needed to survive... Spiritually.

Some find it in accomplishments

Some find it in family

Others, the desperate ones, find it in the soil of which they walk: Countries, states, cities and streets are what they cling to, to find some sense of belonging.

But people who cling to the generality of a certain municipality

As if they were born of the dirt that they define as their own

Are the people without anything at all.

Except an indifferent city

Filled with people prideful of things much more meaningful and fulfilling than a sign that says "city limits"

Walk Along the Waterfront

The soles of my shoes meet the cracked concrete of the city's streets.

Tall lights supplement the sun's absence.

The only natural light left is the moon

Music enters my ears and escapes my headphones

Allowing my personal playlist into the life of others, if nothing more.

You may not know me, but you may know this song

Bonds built on mutual experience is a nice reminder that you're not alone.

Even if you're walking alone.

There's someone out there humming your song.

Allowing the lyrics to escape from their lips

Just to be heard

Can you hear them?

Cats Are Cool

I stared at the ceiling

As I often did

There was no purpose to the day

But then...

My cat sat on my left shoulder

And licked my forehead

His tongue felt like moist sandpaper

He purred loudly

I felt his body vibrate beside me

Big earthquakes tumbling out of his small feline frame.

He stopped licking

And repositioned his body

His tummy sat horizontally on top of my head

His paws dangled by my ears

I started laughing

He didn't know it

But in that dark room

He provided just enough light.

For me to see the purpose of it all.

If only for a day.

You Can Do It Here

I know that it's out there.

I feel it inside of my elastic skin

You have something they want

And many things they don't

Don't lose sight of that.

The birds' eye is the purveyor of a long fall

The concrete is harder the higher you go

The nuance of the characters below is frightening

A blurry mess of faces unseen

Voices unheard

And fears unwarranted

You can't understand the ground until both feet are planted upon it

The sky is empty

The world is full

Yet our wishes are wasted on where the clouds dwell

An empty void of colors that we filled with God

The builders are beside you.

Architects don't go to heaven

They're here, too.

North Star

Surrounded by tall trees is where you'll find the north star.

Skies uninhibited.

Brilliance unobscured.

Waters untamed.

Wild.

Like the soul without the limitations of society.

Pure.

Like the interests of a toddler.

Perfect.

Like the planet, without us.

But I can't be without you.

You, whose laugh bares fruit.

Whose eyes hold the hues of the ocean.

Whose presence could set the forest ablaze.

In the fog, I see things clear.

I take a deep breath.

I've made it.

There's nothing to fear

DON'T LITTER, ASSHOLE

The glow of the urban landscape was darkness masquerading as light. Phallic structures planted where trees once stood symbolized the possibilities of American ingenuity. But it was all a fraud. Skyscrapers darkened the night sky.

Perpetual growth minimized our humanity to just another resource. The city moved fast, yet the traffic moved slow. I wanted to be accepted by these Goliaths. I wanted to conquer them. I wanted to gain their favor. As I've gotten older, their favor became next to worthless.

I looked at the city from a hill. I watched the fog settle and the buildings became visible. I felt uneasy as if I were looking into the vacant eyes of a corpse. I sat on the hood of my car. I enjoyed the breeze and watched the goosebumps on my arm as they greeted the chilly air brought in by the Pacific. I sipped my beer. It tasted like shit. They all tasted like shit. I emptied the can and threw it as hard as I could, but the wind blew it back at me. I caught the can and smiled.

And on the last day, the Lord said "don't litter, asshole."

Sacramento, San Francisco & San Jose

I hate that I hurt you.

I want to be the comfort

But I know I am the cause.

You were more than enough.

You are more than enough.

I can't feel an ocean breeze without thinking about you.

Your eyes

Your faded lipstick on a handwritten note that ended with the word Always...

Your thoughtful gifts

And the gift of your presence

As we drove to the Golden Gate Bridge

And we played E-40 & Mac Dre

You watched me happily as I recited every word

And we kissed

And my heart skipped beats

And when it wouldn't stop you held me

We drove around the city

Inspired

The day ended with

Ewing and Masonic

Nightfall and Nirvana

You & I

And then it was just I

And I became painfully aware

Of how alone

I am.

Sex & Economics

Love is a human concept
But it is often truly realized
By the inhuman
The small minded
And the big hearted
In the big cities
Where the concrete and steel
Combine
To bend the world
To the will of us
We see them
When a man sits in the rain
On the wet sidewalk
Under the awning
Who is often beside him?
His pet
His dog shivers beside him
Growls at the menacing
Inspects the unfamiliar
And eats only when there is enough
That is love
The rest is sex and economics

Don't Try

The classrooms didn't create you.
They couldn't have.
Repetition of the same tired texts can't cultivate brilliance

Nor equate to it.

They only stifle the ability to be added to those lists later on.

The bars created you.

The sour stench of stale piss and warm booze created you

The longing to live a life away from the 40-work week in a warehouse or a post office created you.

The crater-faced fool of Hollywood's flop houses

The drunken factotum of feature length films

The degenerate gambler whose paycheck was as likely to be spent on a losing horse as was to be wasted on a loser's life.

The poet laureate of San Pedro

The man with the beautiful eyes

Bukowski...

Charles Bukowski.

Here's to another 100 years.

Give 'em Hell

And remember

Don't try...

Sacramento Is Not Coastal

When I want to escape the heat of the Sacramento Valley

A place only 60 miles from home

But a world away

From a silly little area that sits on the San Francisco Bay

I google communities on the Pacific Ocean

Small towns.

Coastal nowheres

Filled with foggy nothings

But

Small town diners

Airports so insignificant that they can only support one plane at a time

And the occasional protester tied to a tree

I envision myself there.

I can almost feel the cool air fill my lungs

Then I exhale

And I'm not.

THE ARTIST

PROLOGUE

I knew that if I didn't make it by the age of thirty, I was going to blow my fucking brains out. Not kill myself. No. The idea of saying "I'm going to kill myself" or "I'm going to commit suicide" felt too vague to me. I wanted to leave a vivid image in your mind's eye.

My brains.

Blown out of my skull by a bullet.

It'd have to be done with a large caliber bullet, too. Not some pansy .9, but a .45. Something that would paint the walls. I wanted the piece to have an abstract quality. An impactful suicide should always toe the line between an authentically avant-garde aesthetic and the most extreme elements of performance art. It should have meaning. It should be beautiful, despite the dreariness of death.

I felt that if the world didn't discover me and my art before my faded youth forced my hand into drastic finality, my grand finale must also leave a great first impression. Value is created by scarcity, and the importance of great artists are also measured in scarcity, the scarcity of their lives which lends infinite energy to their works.

I was determined to receive my roses. Even if I weren't around to smell them, the world would smell them for me. The aroma of my decomposing corpse would fill their nostrils, and the essence of my spirit would capture theirs.

Vicarious immortality.

CHAPTER ONE

When I was a child, I was fascinated with colors. Colors controlled the world, every modern institution, held in high regard as pillars in this experiment. This experience we dub humanity was just extrapolation and interpretation on the natural color-coding we inherited from this life-sustaining planet. Cycles, shifts, seasons, and our understanding of those changes were all deeply intertwined with our perception of color. In the truest sense of the word, To be God-like was to be someone with an understanding and command of colors. Any complexity debated by scholars and enforced by men who never held an interest in the rich world of academia, but were continually conned by academics into doing their bidding, could be immediately simplified and understood by color. Good and evil, life and death, partisan politics, gangs, boys and girls, when to eat, when to fuck, what to wear, all of it... was assigned a hue.

My first experience with a man who could control color and create the world was through television, man's greatest mind control device, and docility dispenser. He didn't look like a man of immense power, but he had it. No one with an ounce of uncertainty in their fragile heart could have behaved in such a calm manner. Calmness isn't a mind-set. Confidence isn't a belief in one's ability. It's a symptom of power. I observed this at the age of five and spent much of my life digesting it. My parents placed me in front of the TV to watch a man create the Heavens above and the Earth below in less than thirty minutes. His name was Bob Ross. His hair was untamed. A perfect circle of curly brown hair rested upon his head as if it were a halo. His beard was trimmed but never manicured. His eyes held the darkness of the night sky but shined with the brightness of the stars that penetrated it. He was a man for much of his life, and, like men inevitably do, he died, but when I was a child, sitting there, amazed at how effortless he made his creations appear, he was God.

I wanted to be God, too.

He died roughly three years after my birth. I never was able to appreciate his godliness while he still walked this realm. I discovered the power of color at birth. Every human does, even if they don't know it. However, through my exposure to him, I learned of our ability to control it. In an attempt to momentarily alleviate the burden of raising me, my parents gave me a gift they never intended to provide. It was the only thing that they gave me. It was the only thing that mattered.

It started with crayons and coloring books. Coloring books are a lot like life; you're given an outline, but you choose how the blank spaces are filled. The problem with life is that not everyone is given a fair amount of crayons to achieve the shade that best suits their soul.

Worst of all, it seemed there was always someone exploiting what was missing from your palette in an attempt to add to theirs.

$600: That's what it costs to sleep on the top bunk of a bunk bed illegally placed inside of a warehouse in West Oakland. It's an artist community. Well, not really. Very few artists are here. There are some, but they don't make up the majority. Most are mentally ill burnouts who doodle some-times and obsess over certain bands or other successful, sometimes forgotten creatives. They're dreamers. They don't create, and the people who profit from them by estab-lishing these illegal warehouse dwellings aren't landlords - an already parasitic yet accepted part of our society; they're dream extortionists. It stings more. Most of the people in these warehouses aren't from Oakland, yet they say that they are. They believe that cities, places, and things give art life. They're wrong. Souls do that, but they don't have souls, so they don't know. Even if I told them, they still wouldn't know. For some, some things are just... unknowable.

I was from Pleasant Hill. Born in Oakland, still from Pleasant Hill. Never lied about it, never had to. Pleasant Hill was a subtle compromise between three cities: Concord, a blue-collar suburb; Walnut Creek, an upper-middle-class suburb that pretended to be a rich one and Martinez, a small industrial town that doubled as Contra Costa's county seat. It was basic suburbia. The streets were quiet; there was a community college that people all over the East Bay attended, bringing more life to the streets than cities of similar size. It wasn't gritty. There were no rust-covered buildings or barbed wire fences. It was just a place where people slept after working in cities with all the things it lacked.

Many of my bunkmates were from Pleasant Hill, just under a different name. Despite the faux nature of some of the origin stories I encountered while residing in these "artist" communities, I did appreciate the freedom these spaces allowed me to create. I could paint wildly with uninhibited brush strokes. Color blessed the concrete without consequence. The sweet aroma of marijuana filled the air, and the stench of booze on the breath of those near me filled my heart with nostalgia for my cross-faded teenage years. It was blissful in its own stupid way.

Painting was often a solitary experience; even in artist communities, it was rare that others would show interest in what you were working on. However, in my experience, there was an exception: Sarah Guttierrez. I remember Sarah would question the reasoning for each color I chose. It made me feel like I was being interviewed. It made me feel important. "Why do you always do red?" She would ask. "No matter how many paintings you do, there's always hella red."

"I never really thought about it, but I guess because red is passionate. I'm passionate about my art, so I put red in my art to symbolize that."

"What is the color of serenity?" She asked with smiling eyes.

"Definitely blue."

"So why don't you ever put blue in your paintings?"

"I don't know."

"All that passion, but no peace, huh?"

"Peace is the goal."

"Peace should never be a goal. I think peace is a constant state of radical acceptance. Embrace yourself as is, and I think we'd see a lot more blue in your paintings."

If only she took her own advice.

I used to love to show my work to Sarah. For most of my years as a painter, I was rarely inspired to paint people, but something about her made me want to capture her on the canvas. She had long black hair with a gray streak that she was self-conscious about but only enhanced her beauty. Her mother was Irish, and her father was Mexican. She had deep-green eyes and reddish-brown freckles below them. She had grace to her, even when she was drunk, which, unfortunately, was entirely too often. She made the other drunks food; she made me food, too. She was the mother of the group. Even her bunk bed had a beauty to it. She put flowers on the bunk posts and lit incense to combat the smell of stale liquor and industrial pollution that drifted in from the busy ports nearby. And she, unlike the others, was actually from Oakland. She was a punk and described herself as "brutally honest," but nothing was brutal about her. She was just a nice person who cared for others and wasn't entirely prepared for the world. So, like so many others who aren't ready for the actualities of life, she altered it with alcohol. A lot of alcohol... It wasn't a rare sight to see empty bottles of vodka beside her on the bed as she slept. She didn't drink like the others. She wasn't trying to enhance or romanticize life but escape it entirely. I never did a painting of her.

CHAPTER TWO

First Friday. On the first Friday of every month, a few blocks of Downtown Oakland essentially became a flea market for artists. The city was behind it. First Friday allowed people who would otherwise never step foot in Oakland to "experience" Oakland's culture, all while surrounded by an intentionally visible police presence. There was music and dancing; middle-aged white people dressed like they were going to a high school reunion pretending to have a great time. It was all there. I was there, too. Every month, I filled my truck with paintings to sell to yuppies. I added words to some of the pieces. "EQUALITY" "JUSTICE" Things like that. They like things like that. If you have a painting purchased in Oakland hanging on the wall at your home in Marin, or Walnut Creek, or Palo Alto, or wherever, and the word "equality" is on it, you have successfully atoned for your ancestors' sins. You're good. You can call the police again. You were in Oakland buying art; after all, you can't be that bad. Capitalism was good; it just needed a few tweaks. You're a registered Democrat. You're a good person. In your house, you believe: Black Lives Matter, No Human is Illegal, Love is Love, Women's Rights are Human Rights, Science is Real, Water is Life, Injustice anywhere is a threat to justice everywhere... Thank you for your purchase.

There was this kid from West Oakland I became friendly with. He was 14 or 15, and he was a hustler. He'd seen a lot of shit. He never talked about it, so I'm not sure what he had seen, but you could feel it. He was a friendly kid. He had a sharp sense of humor. We became friends because he made fun of me as I was moving my shit into the warehouse.

"Oh shit! A white boy. Moving into a warehouse in Oakland? And he does art? Brand new. Never been done before! Give this man an award. Wokest white man on the planet. He said, 'fuck you, Mom! You don't understand me. I'm gonna listen to alternative Jazz and drink hella coffee and live next to hella ni**as.' Well, until the landlord kicks us out because y'all got more money than us, but it's cool. Hope you enjoy Oakland, bitch." I started laughing.

"Okay, were you listening to the conversation I had with my mom? Because that is verbatim what I said. How the fuck did you know?" He started laughing. We both were laughing. He still hated me. Not me exactly. He liked me; He hated what I symbolized. I understood it. I moved into his neighborhood by choice, not a government mandate. Now, grandchildren of the people who created the Hell he was forced to deal with are taking his neighborhood. I could still live with my parents, but I had nowhere else to go while following my passion for art. I understood the hate, but my hand was forced. At least, that was how I chose to rationalize my decision.

Not long after moving to Oakland, I started selling my paintings during First Friday. It was the most significant event in the Bay for local artists to sell their work. When it came to sales, it was relatively hit or miss. Some days I made a lot of money; other days, I felt like my work was invisible.

However, I learned one valuable lesson: the profitability of white guilt. A genuinely essential skill for any starving artist seeking to make a living in Oakland. One particularly slow Friday, I was standing on Telegraph for nearly three hours while people walked by my pieces without even a second glance. I noticed a crowd of people buying art from a group of kids, black and brown kids, from one of the schools in Oakland. Despite the advantages in life my whiteness had given me, I felt a rage building inside. The art wasn't very good. And the people who were purchasing the art were all upper-middle-class white people. It was strange. Even though I knew they were strangers, I felt like they had all co-ordinated and agreed upon some kind of mutual plan. There were several artists of color at First Friday, but for some rea-son, none of their art, which was objectively better than the shit these middle schoolers were selling, was generating any real attention. Across from me, I noticed a merchandise booth for The Black Panthers, a cultural and political institu-tion in Oakland, but they didn't seem to be doing any better than me.

At first, I found this profoundly confusing, but upon reflection, I realized that these people weren't interested in buying art; they were interested in feeling good about them-selves. They didn't want to purchase pieces from a white art-ist because they were insecure about their ally status. They also didn't want to interact with a Black Panther or anyone who would potentially challenge their armchair intellectual bullshit. They weren't interested in creativity. They had no interest in political change. They wanted to appear virtuous. They wanted to tell their friends about how they supported these poor children in Oakland. They wanted to feel like they were making a change without changing anything at all. They gave me an idea. It was a sleazy idea that filled my bank account with cash and my soul with shame. Money and self-hatred are strange bedfellows, but bedfellows nonetheless.

I was walking down Willow Street, and I saw the kid who was roasting me again. He was sitting on his bike, staring off in the distance. I approached him.

"Hey, can I, uh, ask you a question?"

"No, I don't want to be in your groundbreaking, barrier-shattering documentary about the life of 'urban youth' in Oakland,' he sneered.

"Well, I'm not a filmmaker, and if this was a film, we're at precisely the part where we have a tense conversation about race. Then we find common ground in some culturally universal thing - probably sports, and then the uplifting R&B song slowly builds for emotional impact.

After that, the scene would probably cut to you sitting at a dinner table with hella white people, presumably my family. The camera focuses on your face too, ya know, emphasize how puzzled you are by the number of forks we have while my mom with blonde hair looks at you with maternal love in her eyes."

"I hate those movies, man."

"Yeah, me, too. So, you fuck with The Warriors? Steph Curry is raw, huh?"

"Bruh, shut up. You're hella stupid," he said with a smile on his face.

"I know. I have a proposition for you that could help us both make some extra money."

"I'm listening," he said as he turned his head toward me. It was the first time we actually made eye contact. He had sad eyes. I didn't like looking into his eyes. They made me feel like something cruel was at play, and there wasn't an escape. You can get trapped in those eyes. I tilted my head down and placed my hand above my eyebrows as if the sun was bothering me.

"So I'm a painter, and I think it would be a cool idea if we worked on stuff together."

"You want me to help you paint?"

"No. I want you to help me sell my paintings at First Friday. I'll give you fifteen percent of whatever we make."

"I want twenty," he immediately replied.

"Deal. What's your name?"

"T."

"What does that stand for?"

"The letter T."

Okay... What's your number?

"510-925-1991"

I programmed his information into my phone and texted him, "sup." He got the text message.

"What's your name?"

"Brad."

"Alright, bye, Brad," he said as he slowly pedaled away.

And just like that, it began...

CHAPTER THREE

Getting used to sleeping in a warehouse on a bunk bed wasn't easy, but it became more challenging due to a reoccurring dream.

I dreamt of a boxer. He didn't have arms or legs. He had large pectoral muscles and defined abs but no arms or legs. His manager just propped him up in the corner of the ring. Beside the limbless boxer was a pair of heavily worn boxing gloves. The bell rang, and the other fighter would approach. The limbless boxer's manager would begin screaming, "get in there!" he said, "this is what we've been training for!" And the limbless boxer would start to take punches. His face quickly became bruised and bloodied, and the first round would end with a roar of applause. Everyone cheered as if both boxers had arms and legs, but only one did. The ringside medics would treat the limbless boxer's wounds while his manager's screams sprayed a mist of saliva over his battered face. The bell rang a second time, and the second round began. However, the second round was much different than the first. When the full-bodied boxer started to walk toward the limbless boxer, confident in his ability to deliver another beating, the limbless fighter surged toward him through some type of supernatural force that I didn't quite understand. The crowd didn't appear shocked by this; they cheered even louder. The limbless boxer began to bite his opponent savagely. He didn't have regular teeth. He had what resembled the teeth of a shark. And blood-like substance sprayed from his opponent's wounds, but it wasn't red like blood; it was jet black.

Black ink-like blood splattered wildly, soaking both fighters. The limbless boxer ripped the flesh from his opponent's neck, causing a wild spray of arterial blood. His prey stumbled, then fell flat onto the mat. The limbless fighter kept chewing. Coaches, managers, and collective members from both fighters' entourages struggled to pull the limbless fighter off. The cheers from the crowd became shrieks of horror. They eventually dragged him back, but it was too late. The other boxer was dead. Lying there, lifeless on the mat. The limbless boxer's manager started weeping, "why did you do that, you fucking monster!" That's where the dream always ended. I'd wake up to the darkness of the warehouse and the sound of the wind. I was often unable to fall back asleep until sunrise.

Not long after making a deal with T, I began having trouble painting. Something about using an underprivileged kid to sell my art emptied me of my passion. Luckily I had several unsold pieces. I just added social justice buzzwords to them. I had no idea it would work or not, but I had a legitimate hunch, and that's better than having no hunch at all. I decided to make a name for the collection. I made a big banner that said, "THIS TREE HAS ROOTS: OAKLAND ART FOR LIBERATION." I was going to have T claim to be the artist. I could feel the money leaving the yuppies' wallets. I felt myself get excited for a second, then I felt like a fraud. I wondered if I was wrong.

I thought to myself, what if it doesn't work? Then I would not only be a fraud but a failure. A fraudulent failure is the worst thing you could be in America. Fraud is okay, but only if you win. That's how presidents are made. Fraud if you lose, on the other hand, well... that's how prisoners are made. Even honest failures could end up in chains. It's not the deceit but the lack of success that made their blood boil. Failure wasn't looked at as a personal problem but a challenge to the continuity of the United States. To its very existence. It's you or them. And while there may be a lot more Yous than Thems, the Thems control all the things the Yous need to become Thems, so even the Yous will be used against you for the benefit... of Them.

CHAPTER FOUR

I had 40 paintings ready to sell. It was a week before First Friday, so I messaged T, not to see if he was willing to be my salesman but to see if he was ready to be my lie. I had informed him of my plan. There wasn't any vague language. I explained that I wanted him to pretend to be the artist; I had witnessed financially comfortable white people buy shitty art because they thought a young disenfranchised youth made it. While explaining all this, it made me feel worse. I began venting to him. I told him I questioned the ethics of such a partnership. I asked him if he felt used by me. I didn't know how he would respond, and he certainly took his fucking time, which increased my anxiety, but once he did reply, he understood what I was saying nearly a day later and agreed to do it. He didn't directly answer my question. His only response was, "LOL." I didn't text back.

There was this park with a fishing pier in Richmond I'd visit to clear my head on days when the warehouse walls were too cramped, and Oakland felt too much like a city for a place nicknamed 'The Town.' The park had a direct view of

San Francisco's skyline. I didn't like looking at San Francisco from a place like Richmond. It felt disrespectful. San Francisco didn't look like a collection of architecturally brilliant buildings placed gracefully on hills that seemed to rise above the heavens from a place like Richmond. 'The City' looked like a set of crude monuments, celebrating the winners of a great war that never truly seemed to end that were symbolically placed in the sightlines of an overflowing graveyard for the casualties on the losing side of the very same conflict.

The breeze was nice, though. I liked watching the dads fishing with their sons while their daughters ran up and down the pier in dresses and sandals - blowing bubbles and giggling. I enjoyed watching the older couples walk the trail near the dock with their sunglasses and visors and smile at passing children. I liked the blueness of the water, and I liked the straight line of fog that managed to burst through the crack in the Earth that we all somehow decided to call the Golden Gate. There were a lot of things to like about this park. I stood on the pier, leaned forward, and thought about everything I wanted. I wanted the recognition of the beauty I saw in colors. I wanted them to see things with new eyes. Eyes given to them by me. I looked to my left and stared at UC Berkeley's clocktower, jutting above the trees; directly ahead was San Francisco and the Bay Bridge. To my right was Mt Tamalpais: the crown jewel of Marin. I thought about my paintings and my bunk bed and the $600.00 I paid to be there. The 'what I had to do' to be on the outskirts of greatness. What I sacrificed to wake up cold in Heaven's own slice of Hell. What I did to convince myself it was worth it. It all came back to me, and I smiled. I couldn't help but smile.

CHAPTER FIVE

Friday. The Friday. The first one. Not the first one ever, but the first First Friday with T. I didn't know if he was a man of his word. I nervously suspected that he wouldn't show up as I loaded my truck with painting after painting. Each one carrying a little piece of myself, each scarred with phrases to appease the simple minds of the symbol minded. I reserved an ambitiously large space along Telegraph. It set me back a few hundred dollars. I guess I did it as a sign of faith in my idea. If you can't find faith in God, find faith in intuition. We have to make a religion out of something, after all. You may as well see it within yourself. At least you know what you worshipped existed at some point, and that's a luxury God's followers can't relate to. They may have Heaven, but you have yourself. Worry about the rest later. You'll have plenty of time, trust me.

I was restless. I had ingested an unhealthy amount of caffeine to keep my mind alert. I woke up the night before at around 3 AM to the same dream of the limbless boxer, but there were some differences in this particular iteration. The black blood used to be proportional to the wounds on the fully-limbed boxer's throat. This time the blood kept coming. The ring was entirely covered in gore. It dripped from the canvas onto the floor below. The screams were louder, the teeth were bigger, almost cartoonishly so. I hated seeing it. I felt responsible. In a sense, I was. It was my dream, but I wasn't in control. It was also the first time I saw fear in the fighter's eyes as he was being eaten alive. I wanted to help him. The brutality of his death made me forget that he was the bully. He agreed to fight a boxer without arms or legs, something only a sociopath would do. He deserved something terrible to happen to him, but not that bad. Barbarism has always found a way to create justifications for bullies, consequently transforming them into victims.

I got to Downtown Oakland at around noon. Telegraph hadn't been closed yet, and vendors weren't allowed to set up until 3 PM. I paid for an all-day parking pass and parked my truck in front of a large mural celebrating Oakland's history. It looked new and uninspired. Commissioned pieces that specifically catered to a city's requested themes always looked weird to me. Any art that celebrated Oakland without acknowledging the reality of Oakland's follies smelled of real estate interests and opportunism, but who was I to complain? Why be an urban haven for the working class when you can transform your city into "West Coast Brooklyn?" I hated money, but I hated the people who had it more than I hated the pointless paper it was printed on. Numbers, fucking numbers printed on paper beside photos of men who meant nothing... controlled everything.

I desperately needed this to work.

Desperately.

CHAPTER SIX

3 PM rolled around, and I began setting up my table. I felt less guilty than I had prior. I felt like I was on the verge of breaking through some kind of barrier placed in front of me by an evil manifestation of everything in life that I despised. A demon smart enough to successfully ruin me for many of my most mundane years but cocky enough to foolishly allow his brain to atrophy -- providing just the right amount of opportunity for me to outsmart him.

T texted me.

"Wya?"

"Downtown setting up, where are you."

"My house u on telegraf, right" How the fuck did he not know how to spell Telegraph? He's fucking from here, I thought to myself. But before I allowed my moment of faux-intellectual superiority to run rampant, I realized that my useless understanding of the fact that some words ending in PH made an F sound didn't make me smarter on any accurate measure of intelligence. It was just an artifact of the fact that academic resources and opportunities tended to be dispersed in school districts populated by the opaque. It had nothing to do with me; it was systemic. I was already an asshole. I didn't need pretension to further alienate me from good karma that may have been generated if I just held open a door for the right old lady. A lady who needed a nicety to lift her spirits after waking up on the wrong side of the wrong bed on the wrong day of the week on the wrong side of the 76-year average American life cycle. At least not when I needed to sell shit. Superstition is at the heart of every risky business venture. The prospect of potentially losing money can make even the most hardened of atheists carry a miniature Bible in their back pocket. God bless America.

Even though it was early, I was antsy for T to arrive. Part of me felt uneasy about putting up the banner I had made without him there. Even if the banner was disingenuous, I didn't want it to look that way. He was my ticket to authenticity. God, I hated myself.

"When are you going to be here???" I paced back and forth around the folding table and roughly 40 or more of my paintings covered with newspaper on Oakland's pavement while waiting for T to respond. After about 30 minutes of avoiding eye contact with every walk of life that happened to walk by, he finally did.

"When does it start."

"It starts at five. Can you head over now??"

"Yea omw."

In order to calm my nerves, I did something out of character. I spotted a dude walking down Telegraph smoking a blunt. He had headphones on, but the cord was just hanging by his left thigh, just below his pocket - they weren't plugged into anything. He had a look in his eye as if he was listening to music. I had no idea if he was or not.

"Hey bro, smells good. Can I hit that?" I said, trying my best to sound cool. He didn't even look at me. He just kept walking, looking satisfied. What a fucking prick, I thought to myself. He was smoking a giant blunt. The aroma hit my nose, and it smelled amazing. I barely smoked weed, but there was something about the smell of marijuana smoked out of a high-quality blunt wrap that made it more enticing.

"Hey," I repeated louder. Still, he didn't look at me. His lips started moving. He looked like he was mouthing lyrics. I walked over to him and tapped him on the shoulder. He slowly turned his head toward me, gave a friendly nod, and took off his headphones only to reveal that he was wearing wireless earbuds. He pulled one out of his right ear. He looked upon me with the warmth of an old friend and said, "What's good, Lion?" I forgot all about the weed for a second and asked, "Why do you wear the wired headphones when you're listening to music on wireless earbuds?"

"Ahh, Lion, I'm glad you asked, bro. I wear the headphones to keep the earbuds from fallin' out."

"But why not just listen to the headphones then?"

"Listen, Lion; life is all about progression, ya feel me? If you can't keep up with the times, you get left in the past. You can't stay activated if you an archive."

"So, the weed's good, huh?"

"The loudest, my Lion."

"I'm having a somewhat anxious afternoon. Can I hit it? It smells hella good."

"Listen, my Lion, between you and me; life ain't free. In a country built on the backs of slaves, creating a caste system, we dub the American Dream - an invisible line segregating prosperity from poverty. Distracting us with a concept of simplicity called ethnicity, you know you gotta have five on it if you tryna' hit this tree."

I started laughing. "That was pretty good. Are you a poet?"

He smiled and said, "And you know I know it." I pulled a crumpled five-dollar bill out of my pocket and handed it to him. He passed me the blunt. I stared at it for a moment, almost unsure of what to do with it. It smelled as good as weed could smell. I took a hit. It didn't burn at first. I held it in, and then suddenly, my throat felt like it was on fire. I coughed. Saliva flew from my lips, and a bit of snot escaped my nose.

"You got this, Lion. That 'Town' shit hit different, don't it?" he asked with a chuckle. I was still coughing. I didn't respond. I internally had to acknowledge the absurdity of my decision to smoke weed. I don't know why I did, but I did. After finally recapturing my ability to breathe, I wiped the various amounts of liquid and gelatinous goop that escaped from every orifice on my face with the sleeve of my shirt; I hit it again. It happened again - the coughing, the saliva, the snot, and the wiping. But I started to feel it. I felt good. The wonderful weightlessness that accompanied a proper hit of a good Indica strain was upon me. I took one more hit, just for good luck. I didn't cough as hard. My lungs had seemed to adjust to the harshness of the smoke. I went to hand the blunt back to the man of multiple headsets, but he didn't seem to want the blunt back.

"Lion! You keep that shit; you earned it, my G," he said with a smile and a nod. I started to laugh uncontrollably. "You're amazing," I said. The weed giggles were in full effect. "Why do you call me lion?"

"Because the world is a jungle, my Lion... And you a lion." He stuck his earbud back into his right ear, and then placed the headphones over them, and began to walk away. After a few steps, he waved his right arm over his head, did the two-fingered peace symbol, and said, "Increase the peace and never talk to police, my Lion." And just like that, he was gone.

Half of the blunt was still left. I held it in between my fingers as it burned and stared at it for a moment. I thought of Kurt Cobain. In his suicide letter, he said, 'it's better to burn out than to fade away.' I thought about that as I watched people go about their day- some setting up their booths, others were walking to who knows where to do who knows what. It didn't matter whether we burned or faded because it usually happened slowly, and we never seemed to notice until it was too late. I dropped the blunt as it was still burning down a storm drain where it would be submerged. It wouldn't fade away or burn out; it was going to drown. There's always an alternative. Who's to say which is better?

CHAPTER SEVEN

I was in one of those weird weed trances where you're not necessarily high, but you're still altered and drowsy. My mind was unable to focus. I was sitting at my table on Telegraph, staring at the signs of businesses and the bustle of Oakland. It's not as crowded as San Francisco but somehow manages to feel just as complete. I didn't even notice T as he popped a wheelie just a few feet away on the same bike he was riding when we first met.

"What up, bruh," he said as he pumped the brakes forcing the bike to stop and the front tire back onto the pavement.

"Yooooo, you made it."

"So what are we doin'?"

"Just living, my Lion!"

"Lion? Is that like some kind of replacement for sayin Nigga?"

"... I... No. I smoked weed with this guy... I'm high," I confessed, "it doesn't matter. And, yeah, I need your help setting up the banner."

I stood up

"Actually, can you set up the banner while I go to the truck and grab some paintings?"

"Sure." I handed the folded banner to him. He unfolded it on the table and started laughing.

"This tree has roots, huh? Hahaha. I hate your ass."

"I know."

CHAPTER EIGHT

T and I finished setting up the banner, and Telegraph Avenue started to come alive. People flooded in from BART stations, cars, on foot - they were everywhere. First Friday

didn't officially begin for another 15 minutes, but it was al-
ready getting packed. T looked at me and asked, "So what do
you want me to do?" I didn't know. I told him just to start
propositioning people and act like he was the artist, and I
would pretend to be an enthusiastic supporter that was
simply happy to be there. I suddenly wasn't confident that
this was going to work, but he was a natural. He had an air
of confidence about him - the way he approached the crowd,
he was magic. T walked up to a white dude wearing khaki
shorts and a black T-shirt - a pair of what appeared to be gas
station aviators hung loosely on the collar. I hated him. I
dressed similarly to him.

"Excuse me, when you think of Oakland, what do you
think?" T continued, "you don't have to say a word because I
already know the answer. You think of crime, death, destruc-
tion, and dysfunction. And shit, excuse my French, but
maybe to an extent that's true, but every change needs to
start, and you can't spell start without art, ya feel me?"

The man smiled and asked, "Are you selling art?" T
pointed to my table and said, "everything you see there is
the product of everything I've ever seen."

I was impressed; the man in the khakis was, too. And
just like that, we sold a fucking painting, and the festival
didn't start for another 10 minutes. He bought the cheapest
painting I had. It was titled "an ocean without the sun." It

was a simple piece, but it had a lot of meaning to me. I was sad to see it go. Despite it being my idea, I was disappointed that this man thought T's were the fingers behind the brush strokes. The painting was on a small canvas. I had painted the background, Mars Black. Waves of Davy's Grey rippled across the canvas outlined in a heavily muted Phthalo Blue. The inspiration that created the particular painting came back to me. I was standing on the end of the pier where Seawall Drive meets University Avenue in Berkeley. It had to be around 1 AM, pitch black aside from the glow of San Francisco's skyscrapers. I looked toward the reddish-orange pillars of the Golden Gate Bridge - perpetually lit, always visible, but the ocean directly to the west of it was gone. The water had been blackened into obscurity by the Sun's absence. I continued to stare beyond the natural borders of what the light allowed, and the waves appeared to me. They were a very dark grey and danced with the motion of the wind. It was like the ocean was conscious of my gaze and made an attempt to manifest only to satisfy my longing to behold its beauty illuminated by nothing but the light in my eyes. But ultimately, my little pact with the sea made $50.00.

"Bruh, did you see the way I finessed that shit?"

"Yeah, you're doing good," I replied with a flat tone. I had a headache. I shouldn't have smoked weed. I was drowsy, and everything seemed to annoy me. I stared at the

crowd passing by, and my eyes lost focus and began to wa-
ter. I looked down at the cracks in the concrete. Even those
were designs to me. The scars of civilization stamped be-
neath our feet. T grabbed one of my paintings - held it in his
hands for a prolonged period. His eyes scanned the piece
from top to bottom. He looked at me and said, "I really like
this one." The piece was called "within arm's reach." It de-
picted a large graveyard, but instead of tombstones, an arm
stuck out of the ground for each body buried. Even in death,
they wanted to be reassured that their lives weren't wasted.
The tiny hands of dead children wilted beside the frail arms
of the elderly. In different stages of decomposition, the limbs
pointed directly at the sky like antennas ready to receive a
radio signal from Heaven. Fingers stretched out, firm with
rigor mortis, all waiting for a final embrace that wouldn't
come. The living mourn the dead but can't hold their hand
and walk them through the process. They have to walk
through it alone. Every color, every single body, an arm
raised. We're all accounted for in the dirt. Equality did exist;
you just had to die for it.

I Left for a Reason

Back and forth

Sacramento and Vallejo

Up and down the I-80 corridor

Caught in the crossfire

Between the flat heat and the mountainous breezes

Between the dysfunction and affordability.

Between the practicality of compromise and the yearning to be home.

I'm on my way home, but I can't stay long.

I left for a reason.

In the Way

Behind the Hitlers and the holocausts

The truth and the lies

The pain and the pleasures

The rich and the poor

The smiles and the cries

The capitalist and the communist

The authoritarian and the libertarian

The dopamine derivatives

The insufficient serotonin

The isolation you feel

And the alienation from your dreams...

Is just a bunch of people.

Perpetually in the way

Of absolutely everything

For reasons next to nothing

The Moral Hubris of the Hills

The beneficiaries of every wrong now gatekeep what is
right.
They sit comfortably in their homes.
Itty bitty boxes that appreciate on tree-lined streets
Perched high in the hills with views of everything and every-
one they own.
They've gone to college.
They've read some books
and boy...
are they eager to help.
They're saving the world.
They recycle.
They bought a Prius
They have a sign that says some stuff.
And they never laugh in public.
They can't
They've been caught red-handed
Because the redlines that their grandfathers painted on
maps still ensure that the neighbors will most likely look like
them
They feel really bad about it
So bad that they never move.
They don't live beside the people they advocate for
They don't even know them.
They can't
Because decorations are meant to be seen
Not heard.

It Won't Save U

If you think the City will save you, it won't.

The dive bars won't increase your depth.

Nor will the bars on the windows keep the bad actors out

And it certainly won't keep the good ones in.

The electric car drivers with the coexist bumper stickers can barely coexist with themselves

And the streets smell like piss.

You probably won't make it

It's hard to stick out in a place where it's all been done before

And it has been done before...

And will be done again and again

Because the grass will never be greener on the other side

If the drought is coming from within.

Performance Art

I don't read poems

And I don't like poets

I don't like people who think a bag being blown a few feet down the street by a breeze is meaningful

Or artistic

I don't like people who call themselves artists

People who call themselves artists

Rarely make art.

They just buy clothes

And move to big cities

To be around more people

Who also

Buy clothes

From people
Who don't make art

Sacramento

I felt trapped in Sacramento
But the words flowed freely.
I would spend hours on Trulia, looking at places I couldn't afford.
Or read about things I couldn't do.
With people I didn't know.
And I'd write.
I'd sit for hours in my warm room
In a place I hated
And I'd do what I loved
To make it all bearable.
I'd read.
I read several books during that duration I spent there
All cooped up in the capitol.
Breathing in wildfire smoke.
Drinking good coffee with great friends
Who never made me feel weird for letting hours turn to days
staring at the ceiling, not saying a word.
Preoccupied with people who meant nothing
I'd read Bukowski
Listen to lofi beats
And pretend to sign books and shake hands.
I'd even act out the movements.
An invisible pen would magically appear my in hand

And I'd sign my signature in sloppy cursive, because that's how you're supposed to do it.

I'd write a little personalized note to a faceless fan that didn't exist.

It would be encouraging.

Like the note Paluhniuk wrote for me.

It would say something about not giving up.

Even if the words weren't there.

I'd write them anyway.

I'd write them.

Any way.

I could.

PRODUCTIVE PEOPLE

A SHORT STORY ABOUT LIFE IN A POSSIBLE FUTURE

New York, NY; June 8, 2081

The auditorium was dark. There were roughly 3,000 people in attendance. If you weren't invited, you didn't matter. The most influential business elites from all four corners of the globe were packed into this room. All of them were waiting to hear a keynote address from Dr. Himlaryan. Dr. Himlaryan was unique even by Silicon Valley standards. He was an expert in both neurology and economics. His insights were essential in expanding the business model and ethics of Silicon Valley into every facet of the global economy. Before Dr. Himlaryan, only developed nations had their commercial prowess tracked. Himlaryan introduced algorithms into even the most basic forms of commerce. It didn't matter if you bought something from an online merchant or purchased a chicken from a local farmer in an African village. Dr. Himlaryan found a way to track the data and utilize it to serve digital commerce needs best. However, this was only the first phase of his ambitions. His true obsession was eugenics. He believed that the core idea of eugenics would bear fruit as long as the process of determining human deficiency remained unburdened by America's obsession with skin pigmentation. His focus was on what characteristics existed

within the human brain and how understanding these neu-
rological strengths and weaknesses could increase produc-
tivity for the international business community. For Dr.
Himlaryan, the more we could conceivably produce, the
more we could conceivably become. Profit and evolutionary
potentials were the same to him. And that's why this audito-
rium, filled with the powerful, was so significant. The world
was about to change, and you weren't invited...

A stage light turned on over an elevated podium with
a sign on it that read "**Commercial Consciousness for A New
Global Century**" A hologram of a man in an expensive-look-
ing suit with dark, slicked-back hair was generated just to
the left of the podium.

"Dr. Himlaryan would like to thank all of you for tak-
ing the time out of your busy schedules to attend this event.
The keynote presentation will be approximately one hour in
length. As a precaution to ensure the information discussed
within this presentation remains confidential, all digital de-
vices - including enhancements such as physical, cognitive,
or ocular augmentation must be placed into sleep status. An
electromagnetic pulse scrambler device will be turned on in
the auditorium to disrupt any potential offline recording de-
vices during the duration of the keynote presentation. We
know that it is highly unusual to require a physical presence
in this era of singularity, but this is the only way to ensure

that the ideas discussed here are not exposed to the world without the proper context. We appreciate your understanding and patience. The presentation will begin shortly." The hologram turned around as if it was about to walk off stage and disappeared.

The audience applauded. It was strange. They were given a list of things they couldn't do under the guise that they were about to be given information that would greatly expand the things they could do... in the future, just as long as they followed the list of things they couldn't do in the present. Humanity - even among those described as leaders, they're likely to follow the lead if their "leadership" is acknowledged. People don't change at the top; they relish intellectual ambiguity, tradition, and politeness.

The crowd chattered amongst themselves. Their conversations all revolved around money, status, and seating arrangement. A few commented on the novelty of holding a conference in person. But mostly, they were quiet. The anticipation was palpable. These were people who had gotten anything they ever wanted immediately, and that immediacy was expedited. These people had everything they could ever want before they had the time to think over their desires. So, for many people in the audience, this was a first in more ways than one. With the requirement to turn off their tech modifications and devices, coupled with waiting, many of these people were becoming human for the first time, if only for a few minutes.

A calming female voice came from the speakers at the foot of the stage. "Please welcome Dr. Alexander Himlaryan." Several people in the audience rose to their feet and began applauding, a few stayed seated, but most clapped with an enthusiasm that seemed so intense it appeared inauthentic. Dr. Himlaryan walked to the podium slowly with the confident swagger of a man who understood his ideas would influence the people who influenced everything. He wore dark blue denim jeans, a black T-shirt with white calligraphy that said "longevity" in Japanese kanji. The shirt was made of entirely recycled fabric. The doctor matched it with a blazer, accompanied by a pin that had an image of Nikola Tesla on the left lapel and a black pair of restored leather dress shoes that appeared to have been polished moments before the presentation by the way the stage lights sharply reflected off of them.

Once he made it to the podium, he warmly smiled at the audience as the applause grew louder and the clapping accelerated in speed. He nodded his head at them in agreement with their adoration of his apparent genius.

He leaned his head toward the microphone, and the gold flecks floating in his sea-blue eyes sparkled in the direct light that poured in from above.

"I want all of you to look at who is sitting next to you," he paused for effect and began again, "and understand that you have everything in common with that person.

"Advanced neurological evolution made possible by a perfect storm of genetic opportunity that placed each one of you in a position to achieve supremacy in an economic environment built to promote efficiency and growth. This economic system is global in scope and endless in its complexities as it navigates the nuances of law, borders, languages, and cultures. Not to mention the rapidly expanding digital spaces that augment our bodies, enhance our lives but ultimately leave the majority of our species feeling lost as the march of progression moves faster than they can comprehend. Yet, all of you did comprehend and remained in power despite the technological changes. The world would be better off with more people like you - like us. And that is precisely why we're here."

A chart appeared behind Dr. Himlaryan that showed previous levels of global economic productivity.

"As you can see from this chart, productivity and profits have soared. We have increased productivity and profits year-over-year for the last five years...." The audience began applauding. "Stop," Dr. Himlaryan commanded the crowd with disdain in his voice. "This is not good enough." Another chart showing full economic potential for 2080 appeared behind him.

"We only reached 76% of our projected global economic potential for that year, and nearly 1/4th of what we could've achieved in 2080 was wasted. That is nothing to celebrate, and it's a slap in the face that none of you should accept."

A chart depicting the nucleus accumbens and the prefrontal cortex appeared behind Dr. Himlaryan. "We can consult with every single economist in the world. We can analyze algorithm after algorithm, but the answer to reaching our productivity potential - our true potential is based in understanding the human brain and by extension, the human worker."

Bright lights above the stage pointed at the crowd illuminated the auditorium.

"Look at yourselves. Among you, what do you see? I see familiarity. Do you see differences? We have every hue of skin color, eye color, gender, and national origin in this audience. Yet, despite the odds, you have all superseded expectations. Proving that we have limited our ability to create the ideal human and, by proxy, a better worker, focusing on superficialities that have halted progress. We have to reassess and find the root cause of human degeneration. We have to identify neurological weakness in the global population and humanely eliminate it among all walks of modern life. Only then will those most cognitively fit to carry the torch of the human spirit into the future can do so uninhibited by the unnecessary burden of those unworthy of such a task."

Dr. Himlaryan pointed to the wall behind him, and a live projection of the audience appeared.

"You may appear different on a surface level, but intellectually, this room is among the most homogeneous on the planet. Surface level diversity is an illusion created by adaptations to UV rays and a myriad of other environmental conditions that existed long before we could even be conscious of such differences or their origins. To make a better world, we need to eliminate diversity - neurological diversity to be more specific. We need to eliminate the weak, the poor, and the stupid. Unproductives aren't made unproductive by economic neglect but by intellectual incapacity. Some of you in this very room have come from, out of sheer statistical anomaly, from the weak. The feeble-minded among us can, on occasion, produce a leader, but it's not enough to justify their continued unguided existence in the large numbers they so thoughtlessly reproduce."

A high-quality photo of the earth appeared on the screen behind Dr. Himlaryan.

"So, what do we do? Much of the world has been made uninhabitable by our overpopulation and the resulting rapid changes in climate. Much of the African continent and parts of Central Asia are too hot to live in, not to mention large sections of North America. The western United States is constantly burning. The Silicon Valley and the greater San Francisco Bay Area where I reside is more likely to experience blood-orange skies than it is to be enveloped by the fog that I grew so fond of as an undergraduate at Stanford. The Southern U.S. and Midwest are economic dead zones with unpredictable weather patterns. The Eastern U.S., the place where we have decided to gather today, once a powerhouse of global capital, is on the verge of irrelevance as the digital economy has made the entire concept of location appear antiquated."

Dr. Himlaryan placed both hands on the podium and stared into the crowd. "What do we do?" Could we perpetuate another genocide? I know some of you are reaching that conclusion, but the old methods of genetic reconfiguration are the same as the large buildings that needlessly fill this filthy city: antiquated."

An image of a woman wearing a hospital gown lying flatly in an oval-shaped pod with a smile on her face appeared on the screen. Her eyes were closed. Various tubes, some plastic to sustain hydration and nutrients, others metal to monitor any potential physical or digital augmentations. The word "HUMANE" sat awkwardly in large red letters under the image. For some reason, even without proper context, this image made some of the elites in the audience applaud. The image zoomed out, revealing rows of similar pods with different people; as the image continued, more pods appeared until each pod and the person assigned to them were reduced to unrecognizable dots on the screen.

"Existence should be based on individual merits divorced from surface-level prejudice. In the past, population reduction has been traumatic, based on trivialities, and prone to intense scrutiny from the humanitarian-minded among us. My humane method of genetic molding is based on neuroscience and productivity analysis using the same proprietary SaaS (Software as a Service) that made me a leader in global commerce," Himlaryan paused for effect. Despite his outward confidence, he wasn't entirely confident of the response he would receive to such a radical idea. How does one convince the most influential people to participate in genocide while extolling its virtuosity as the main characteristic? The premise to his argument was that he wasn't killing anyone; he was decommissioning them until they died peacefully of natural causes. Even for Himlaryan, it was a taxing argument to make, but to his surprise, he wasn't met with resistance but intrigue. He stood at the podium quietly, anticipating an objection that never came.

He took an anxious breath and continued. "We all monitor our workers, and when we observe consistent dips in productivity, at first, we speak to them and provide a sort of corrective counseling. This is usually delivered by a manager or someone else we placed as a sort of overseer, but this is ultimately a waste of time. Anyone who consistently wastes finite resources and capital is clearly suffering from a diagnosable deficiency and would likely waste more resources if we attempt to *cure* them of their lackluster traits to varying degrees of efficacy. And that is precisely what I aim to fix."

Himlaryan walked away from the podium and began to pace around the stage. Another image appeared, showing what could be achieved in his ever-improving vision for utopia. It showed children of all races and cultures working jobs at as close to 100% efficiency as possible, all with smiles on their faces. It transitioned to a close-up image of an unproductive worker aging while comatose in a pod... with an ever-present smile. It showed the earth healing from the damage caused by population growth, healing from the ecological scars of war. Trees were becoming more abundant; the west burned less, San Francisco's fog returned, the heat waves and blizzards in New York grew less intense. These images were accompanied by restored audio recordings of Martin Luther King's "*I Have a Dream*" speech. Under Himlaryan's vision, the economy's efficiency would reach near 100%, while capitalism's impact on the world greatly lessened due to a rapidly reduced population. These perfect workers, bred to be the best, though their version of natural selection, by way of humane genocide, would serve the interests of an elite that sat mesmerized in a New York Auditorium. It wasn't enough for them to control the world; they had to feel good about themselves, too. A bunch of Mother Theresas fooling themselves as they arbitrarily "decommissioned" those they deemed didn't work hard enough to justify their existence, which was ultimately to serve them.

Dr. Himlaryan walked back to the podium. "And this is how it will work." He took a deep breath and continued, "We will analyze productivity in each worker; if we notice a decrease in productivity, we will pull them for neurological analysis. We will then find out if they are positive for genetic components that make them more susceptible to things like drug addiction or anything that can be defined as neurodivergent. If these traits are found, we will do a similar analysis on their family. We will go down the line, and each worker will be decommissioned. However, to be decommissioned is not a punishment, but in many ways, a gift. These brain scans will find what stimuli gives them the most pleasure, and in their unconscious state, they will be given just that until their body dies. In the event of a natural medical emergency, we would proceed with a hands-off approach. Just let it happen. Let them die. The pods will assure they will not be in any pain and increase dopamine and serotonin levels to offset any potential pain that may disrupt their co-matose state. Upon death, we will give their body back to the earth. It will fertilize the planet. The planet feeds us; we must reciprocate. No casket, place them in the dirt and let our planet consume, as we have for centuries... Any questions?"

And the people in the auditorium did have questions. Questions regarding implementation.

There were no objections...

****

San Francisco, CA; March 22, 2100

"Good afternoon Mrs. Arnstein. Do you know why you're here?" Asked the doctor.

"I... don't. I was told I had to take a screening and that it was mandatory to keep my job. That's all my boss said."

"I see. Well, I assure you that there is nothing to worry about. This is just an aptitude test. I'm going to ask you a series of questions, and then we're going to do a few painless scans -- mostly neuro scans, but those will occur later."

"What's your name?" Deborah Arnstein asked.

The doctor paused. He tilted his head, and his eyes were momentarily fixated on the sterile white floor.

"As per corporate procedure, we are not permitted to provide our given names due to the anonymity clause in our contract, but I can provide you with my employment code. I am Dr. 0092510-415-707."

"But you get to know my name?"

"As per corporate procedure, we have to. We are trained to create a level of comfort and familiarity with our patients while administering these tests. If I didn't address you by your birth name, I would be in direct violation of the physicians' conduct clause in my contract."

"Are you human?" Deborah paused, "No one's fully human these days, but are you organic spawn, or are you code?"

"As per corporate procedure, I regret to inform you that that type of question is in direct violation of the Martin Luther King clause, which is in every employee contract. If you retain your employment at the end of this test, you will hear from the Conscious Resources department," the doctor replied sternly.

"Did you know that Martin Luther King was murdered while leading a march for the rights of workers? I think it was called the Poor Peoples' or Poor Persons' Campaign, something like that... Don't you think it's weird that a man who died fighting against corporate interests would have a clause named after him in a corporate contract limiting what workers can say?"

"I don't know who Martin Luther King is. I just know there's a clause named that."

Deborah stared at her hands and accepted that this would likely be her last day of real life. She was going to be decommissioned. There were rumors about what happens to unproductive workers or anyone who spoke out; even those meeting their productivity quotas would be labeled unproductive and removed if they questioned the contracts. No one knew where they went, but there were rumors of large metal containers where people would sleep forever, and sometimes their families would go with them. Workers said corporations would "cancel" you. That was the colloquial term for it. People would just disappear. Any aspect of life that didn't match the advertisements would be scrutinized and eventually removed, and those ads were everywhere. The neurolinks infiltrated our dreams with ads. Product placement would even appear in nightmares. The algorithm in the neurolink wasn't advanced enough yet to distinguish between good and bad dreams. To the neurolink, dreams were dreams. Deborah rarely remembered her dreams, but one particular nightmare had made her petition to get her neurolink removed. She was being raped. The man was getting ready to enter, and she begged him to wear a condom. As the rape occurred, a disembodied voice said, "You never know when life is going to happen to you; even when you're not protected, the sex can be. Thin Skin Condoms - keeping the sensitivity intact while making sure you don't contract! Available at *www.quickshop.globe* and all participating retailers!" The petition for the neurolink's removal was denied.

The doctor's eyes glowed an electric blue indicating that his data lens had been turned on. Her chart and the questions he was about to ask were visible only to him.

"We're going to begin the test. Please answer the questions honestly, as the neurolink will pick up on cortisol spikes and other hormonal changes consistent with lying. Please answer every question thoroughly, thoughtfully, and concisely." Deborah gave a slight nod.

"It's a sunny day. You and your family are going to the beach. You receive notification that a storm is quickly approaching, yet you don't see any evidence of an impending storm. Do you: A. Continue your trip to the beach? B. Heed the weather warning and go home. Or C. Contact an official to inquire about the weather."

"I'd continue the trip, and if it rained, I'd just head home."

"Are you saying that you don't trust our Information Alert Corporation's notification system?"

"I'm saying if I was going to go to the beach and the skies were blue if it started to rain, I could always drive home."

"Would you agree that driving in inclimate weather is less efficient than driving in sunny weather?"

"What do you mean?"

"It is common for storms formed in the Pacific to be windy. The higher the wind speeds, the more power the battery must expend to power the car during the drive. Would you agree that it would be better to listen to the information provided by the IAC as it would expend less energy, thus increasing the longevity of the car's lifecycle?"

"I guess?"

"It is now time for the neuroscan," the doctor said abruptly.

"Wait, that's it?"

"The number of questions is dependent upon the responses given."

"Did I say something wrong?"

"We must now advance to the neuroscan portion of the test," the doctor continued, "you may feel a burning or vibrating sensation from your forehead down to your shoulders as we initiate your neurolink's neuroscan function. This is normal. If the pain becomes too much to handle, we can issue a temporary numbing agent and begin the test again."

"Do I have any choice?"

"The test will begin in exactly 60 seconds."

Deborah silently stared at the doctor. His face was pale. He had the look of a 20-year-old but the hands of a much older man. He likely was a YOUTHNOW recipient. YOUTHNOW was a product marketed to the upper classes to make organics appear younger if they decided against going full cybernetic. Cybernetics came with its downsides, primarily in the area of sexual pleasure. While you could preserve your cognitive function by fully digitizing your consciousness, sex could be imitated but never experienced the way you could while still in your organic body. For that reason, many didn't go fully cybernetic and only embraced augmentations instead of a complete cognitive transfer until they sat at death's doorstep. The YOUTHNOW organic cellular therapy was the best way to appear young, but there were certain telltale signs that someone was a YOUTHNOW recipient: their hands. For whatever reason, the hands were unaffected by YOUTHNOW therapy. The rest of the body would reverse in age, but hands retained the appearance of the recipient's natural age.

Deborah could tell the neuroscan had begun. She felt a vibration in the middle of her forehead. The sensation wasn't painful; it was more irritating than anything. The speed of the vibrations increased, and she began to see spots. Tiny purple, green and pink spots appeared at random in her field of vision. A subtle burning sensation radiated from the bottom of her shoulders up to her neck, and she began to sweat.

"How much longer?"

"The neuroscan takes approximately twenty-two minutes and thirty-six seconds to complete."

"How long has it been?"

"The duration will continue as I am delivering this answer, but as of the last review, nineteen minutes and zero seconds, approximately, of course."

Her mind wandered as she sat there, feeling the vibrations pulsate along her eyebrows. She thought of her life, and the days she used to stroll atop the hill just behind her childhood home in Hercules. She could see San Pablo Bay and the twinkle of lights across the water in Marin County. She didn't understand how significant those days were then, the days when singularity was a choice. The days when the air was fresh and your dreams were free from ads. The air wasn't always fresh, and the ads were there every waking moment, but there were brief periods of escape. Now escape is impossible. Your mind in every state was property, and your ability to work was the only thing that guaranteed your next second of unscrutinized existence. There are few things worse than a corporate bureaucracy that never slept or allowed you to.

The vibrations stopped, and the test concluded. The doctor quietly left the room. She went to follow behind him, but the door was locked. She sat back down and began to weep. She wiped the tears from here and quickly composed herself. She waited for nearly an hour before the door opened. It was a man she hadn't seen before. His muscles were large and pushed through his uniform.

"It's time to go."

"I know," she replied.

About The Author

Abraham Woodliff is an Oakland-based writer and the founder of Bay Area Memes, a popular meme page that tackles the challenges of Bay Area living with humor and class consciousness. His writing has appeared on SFGate, BrokeAssStuart.com and The Bold Italic.

PREVIEW OF *THE GHOST OF MERE ISLAND*
A NOVELLA COMING SOON FROM
ABRAHAM WOODLIF

Every town in America has its legends, hauntings, myths, and we're no different. For kids who grew up in Vallejo and Benicia, we had 'The Ghost.' He wasn't a ghost, but a man we called 'The Ghost.' Everyone in town knew of 'The Ghost,' but despite universal knowledge of 'the Ghost's existence, very little information could be verified concerning this man. We knew he was homeless, and he frequented Mare Island, a decommissioned naval base that closed in 1996, which ultimately led to Vallejo's economic deterioration. Benicia, the town I'm from, fared much better. We had the refinery to fall back on. Pollution is a fair price to pay for economic stability; at least, that's what Mr. Evans has said about the presence of the refinery in our small North Bay town.

It was senior year, and our Journalism teacher, Mr. Evans, informed us that our last assignment, worth 30% of our grade, was going to be a profile piece on a significant local of our choice. We would have to conduct interviews with this important local, take their photo, and ultimately "write a story that's worthy of being called news." For whatever reason, Mr. Evans would work that "write a story that's worthy of being called news" line into every one of his class lectures, sometimes more than once. It never really had the impact that I think he had intended. Other than a forced catch-phrase, he was a good teacher. We learned about nut graphs, the inverted pyramid, AP style, and everything else our collective teenage brains could absorb to assist us on our journey to "write a story that's worthy of being called news." Most of the students in the class didn't care about journalism. The room was filled with people who settled because Journalism was one of the last elective classes available, and Benicia High School required that an elective be completed to graduate. Their choices of who to profile reflected this apathy. Many of my classmates picked from a suggestion list passed out by Mr. Evans. You had Benicia Police officers, senior faculty members, business owners, and executives from the refinery who spent their money to keep the lawn of Benicia High School green. What was ironic is that they made their money from mixing chemicals that would eventually turn the grass and our lungs black. It was fucking boring; My story wasn't going to be boring.

"Mr. Evans, do we have to pick from the list, or can we pick someone ourselves?" I asked.

"As long as they're a well-known local and the profile fits the guidelines given, I don't see an issue with choosing your candidate, but it has to be someone of significance to the community. No rappers from Vallejo or rappers from Benicia that say they're from Vallejo. The last thing this profile piece needs to devolve into is a promo tool for some rap group with a corny name like the 707 boys or the Benicia Ballers," Mr. Evans replied.

"While I appreciate your no rap rule, Mr. Evans, if there is a group with the inclination to call themselves the Benicia Ballers, it is an absolute obligation to interview them. Not because of their music, which I'm sure would be... incredible, but to find the underlying source of their bravery."

Mr. Evans stared blankly at me and gave a faint smirk.

The bell rang.

"Remember, AP style! This is not a normal essay, and I know some of you have been struggling with that. My office hours are 4 to 5 PM Tuesdays and Thursdays. If anyone needs help with the profile or any refreshers, that's when I'll be able to devote my time," Mr. Evans announced as most of the class rushed out.

I stayed behind.

I often stayed after class because I was passionate about journalism, and Mr. Evans was one of the few people I could discuss the subject with at length. He wasn't just a teacher; he was a friend.

"So Ben, who are you thinking of covering for the piece?"

"Honestly, someone kinda unconventional.

"Unconventional can be good. Who?"

"You know 'The Ghost?'"

"The Ghost, as in the pale creepy guy that hangs out in Vallejo and pushes a shopping cart filled with random shit and half-finished statues of people? That Ghost?"

"That would be the one."

"Isn't he a rapist or something?"

"People say that. But people say a lot of things about him, and no one really knows anything. I've heard everything from murderer to rapist to Napa State hospital escapee, but no one has any proof. They just say that because he looks weird."

"So, when I assign a project about a significant member of the community, instead of a police officer or a firefighter, you wanna cover a weird-looking homeless man who's famous locally because he looks weird?"

"Yeah, pretty much."

"That's why I like you, Ben."

"Thanks, Mr. Evans."

"Just one thing."

"What?"

"If anyone asks, I didn't know you were planning on covering him, okay? The last thing I need is parents in

Benicia thinking I'm encouraging teenagers to go and hang out in Vallejo, let alone to interview creepy old men in Vallejo."

"I think if I'm going to write a story, it's going to be a story 'worthy of being called news.'"

"Shut up, Ben."

I chuckled

"See ya later, Mr. Evans."

"Be careful, Ben. Sometimes when you chase ghosts, you end up haunted...."

****

The weekend came, but my certainty in my project's subject was waning. As each day moved closer to when I'd have the free time to find and interview 'The Ghost,' I became more hesitant.

I didn't know where to start. How do you walk up to a man who you assume is mentally unstable and ask him questions for a school project?

As I sat in my car, the car that my parents bought me, I felt like a privileged vulture picking at a corpse discarded by a system with insufficient safety nets.

I felt like a piece of shit.

Who was I to shove a camera phone in this man's face and take photos? Who was I to tell his story to a bunch of high school kids who lacked sight of his basic humanity and used his visible despair as a subject for gossip and ridicule?

But I needed to tell his story.

I hated the stigma associated with Vallejo. To me, Vallejo was a city of beauty and childhood nostalgia.

I was born in Vallejo, and up until 5th grade, I lived in Vallejo.

I only knew that Benicia existed in theory. My family and I were Vallejo people. My grandfather worked on Mare Island; he didn't build ships; he was a custodian. He mopped floors, washed toilets, and bought a modest home on Hayman Avenue in East Vallejo after some time. My father grew up in that house. When my grandfather passed away, that house, bought and paid for with years of my grandfather's labor, was left to my father. My father, who should've been grateful to have property handed to him, seemed unsatisfied with the house on Hayman Avenue.

He seemed unsatisfied with Vallejo.

But I loved that house. When I thought of Vallejo, I didn't think of crime or bankruptcy. I thought about walking from my house with my friends to Steffan Manor Elementary school, and the thrill my friends and I got from listening to local rappers like E-40 and Mac Dre. It made me feel cool when I'd hear them mention Vallejo proudly in their songs. It was elementary school, so we didn't know what they were talking about in their raps, but we knew we were from Vallejo, and they were, too. We felt like we were a part of something special, a unique feeling at that age. Or any age, really...

It was at that moment I decided to go ahead with the story. I was nervous, but growth without nerves usually isn't growth at all. I turned the key, heard the roar of the engine, and began my search for a ghost.

To calm my nerves, I decided to take the scenic route from Benicia to Vallejo. I exited the freeway at Columbus Parkway and drove north until I reached where it intersected with Tennessee Street. The view from the top of Tennessee Street was a sight to behold. You could see the entire city from up there. I could see the blue pillars of the Mare Island bridge, the colorful cranes, the transparent fog that settled peacefully on the ever-moving waters of San Pablo Bay. I could see it all.

Most of the eastern half of Tennessee Street was residential. I passed apartment complexes and postwar homes situated under the shade of mature trees. I felt a longing as my car reached Maple Avenue. I walked up and down Maple Avenue as a child when my family and I lived at the old house on Hayman. A part of me wanted to abandon the interview and just drive by the old house a few times, but my dad sold it, and it wasn't ours anymore.

During the seven years that had passed since I moved to Benicia, little about Vallejo had changed. I-80 was still used to divide the city across class, if not racial lines. If they still lived in Vallejo, the middle and upper-middle class tended to reside in the city's eastern half. While there were some exceptions, the majority of the poor and working-class neighborhoods are found west of 80.

Many of the trees that could be seen east of 80 were decidedly absent once you crossed the overpass to the western half of Tennessee Street. Homes were more likely to be in disrepair, and the area became more commercial. You could find predatory check-cashing businesses, tire shops, weed dispensaries, and poorly maintained churches and restaurants that served food from behind bulletproof glass. All of that and more found after the last stretch of tree-lined, quaint suburbia that managed to survive the split just west of I-80. The squalor depressed me as I continued westward to Mare Island.

In what seemed like the blink of an eye, I was approaching the bridge. My anxiety reached a point of crescendo the moment my tires came into contact with the steel in the center of the causeway that produced a loud buzzing noise. The Napa River was far narrower than I had remembered. Or maybe it was always narrow, and my nerves made the typically short trip over the water feel shorter.

Mare Island was still desolate. I heard of some redevelopment efforts, but the only evidence of such plans were the signs zip-tied to chain link fences surrounding the old barracks. The signs announced that the property was in the hands of a developer called the Clemitz Group and that trespassers would be "prosecuted to the full extent of the law" under some obscure California penal code that no one gave a fuck about. The warning felt disingenuous. Anyone who attempted to trespass in the derelict buildings on Mare Island likely fell into one of two categories. First were people who were excited at the idea of exploring the innards of a coastal corpse left by the American Empire. The "full extent of the law" for them would likely be a 'rent-a-cop' telling them to go. Other people were likely those who had so little to lose that the threat of the "full extent of the law" was as about as significant of a deterrent as holding in a fart would be to fight climate change.

I had no idea what I was doing. I aimlessly drove around a peninsula called an island for 30 minutes looking for a man called a ghost. Mount Tamalpais loomed in the western horizon. No matter where I drove, the gaze of Mount Tam felt inescapable. Seeing the natural beauty of Marin County in the distance juxtaposed against the twisted structures left to rot as a result of the artificial catastrophe that befell Vallejo made me feel nauseous. Poverty and prosperity were everywhere in America, but they were often forced into a staring contest in The Bay Area. Behind the veneer of civility on behalf of 'The Haves,' you could see the subtle smirk, reminding you of your place as a have not.

I continued to roam until, eventually, I spotted it: the shopping cart. It was filled with statues of people and trash bags that contained God knows what. Some of the sculptures were close enough to completion that you could make out genders, facial expressions, and age. The statues that appeared to be of children all seemed happy with smiles carved into their faces. The ones that seemed to be of adults seemed to be in pain. Some were remarkable in their attention to detail; others looked rushed, incomplete, and uninspired.

The shopping cart sat unattended beside a large hole in the chain-link fence surrounding a dilapidated warehouse that appeared to have no other purpose but to look menacing.

I pulled to the side of the road and stopped my car. I took a deep breath as the roar of the engine went silent. Brand new bolt cutters leaned against the fence just inches from the hole. I assumed someone may have assisted 'The Ghost' in acquiring such tools. He was too visibly deranged to walk into a local hardware store to purchase, let alone steal tools of any kind. I sat in my car, both hands tightly gripping the steering wheel. I was waiting for any sort of excuse I could deem legitimate enough not to approach this man, to not walk into that creepy-looking warehouse, made accessibly by a suspiciously new set of bolt cutters. Some part of me felt that he was waiting in there for me, butcher knife sharpened, salivating at the thought of slitting my throat. I looked at my cell phone as it sat upside down in my excessively-large cup holder that I assume was made to accommodate America's increasing appetite for 64 oz. soft drinks to wash down their 1/2 pound of heart disease with a side of fries. No calls came, though. No texts. Nothing. No 'get-out-of-jail-free card.' If I backed out, it was on me. The universe seemed uninterested in providing me with excuses. I had to choose. So, I did... I got out of my car and walked through the hole in the fence toward the warehouse.

The crunch of broken glass punctuated each step I took inside the vast warehouse. Trash and debris were everywhere. The walls were covered sporadically with graffiti; some of the pieces had artistic merit. Others were nothing more than scribbles afforded a larger canvas than the crumbled binder paper they usually call home. I knew this structure was at one point used by the Navy, but despite finally being within the building, there was no indication of what its initial purpose may have been.

I continued to move forward until I reached a massive wall with a single door in the middle of it that I instinctively felt would lead me back outside. To my surprise, this large wall divided the warehouse into two sections of similar size. When I opened the door is when I saw them; *hundreds of them*. The statues were everywhere. Some were life-size, others were so small you could place them in your pocket. I wanted to turn around and run, but I didn't. I just stood there, trying to wrap my mind around the number of statues I was looking at. Some were made from wood and looked like they had been carved with nothing more than a kitchen knife. Others appeared to be made from clay. They seemed to be placed around the warehouse at random. As I strolled through the place, I felt a sickness in my stomach. I smelled smoke and heard the crackle of firewood. A hole was in the ceiling at the far corner that let in a beam of sunlight. In the clarity of the sun's partially obscured glow, I could see the smoke. I absentmindedly went toward it, and that's when I saw him: I found 'The Ghost.'

He sat on the ground directly facing the fire; his legs were crossed. He was still, but his shadow danced wildly with the flames. His skin was as pale as chalk, and his long white beard was tan in comparison to the opaqueness of his face. A pile of small wooden statues was burning. I heard him let out a whimper. He was crying...

I just watched. I didn't know what to do. I couldn't have been more than 30 feet away; however, 'The Ghost' seemed unaware of my presence. I felt voyeuristic. I was watching a homeless man cry while he destroyed his possessions — his creations. Relief shouldn't have been the first thing I felt when I witnessed him weep, but it was. When I heard the cries, the sniffles, and the moans, I knew he wasn't a crazed murderer. I knew he wasn't going to hurt me. He was a *person*. He had a *soul*, and he was in *pain*. Just like you or me...

"Are you okay?"

I don't know why I asked; I just did. My mind was silent, and the words just came out of my mouth. He slowly turned his head toward me. His tears became visible; they glowed a fiery orange as they streamed down his cheeks until they settled upon the surface of his beard.

"I am, but they're not," He said. "They were never given a chance to feel the warmth of the sun or the cool air of an ocean breeze. We're complicit. All of us, but some more than others. I, more than others and others more than I."

"I don't understand."

"Yeah, you do. You just don't know that you do."

I began walking toward him. He looked away from me and returned to staring at the pile of small burning statues. As I approached, I felt the warmth of the fire soothe my skin. I don't know where this sudden bravery came from, but it felt natural. I cleared a spot on the concrete of debris with my foot and sat by the fire. I was directly facing 'The Ghost.' He just sat there — eyes focused on the burning pile, tears still streaming down. He was utterly uninterested in my being there. I felt purposeless. I just stared at him. I looked into his mournful blue eyes and couldn't see his pupils; the reflection of the flames hid them. His eyes transfixed me. They were bright and beautiful. With the moisture of his sorrows and the blaze that stoked them, the hue of his eyes was reminiscent of the Pacific ocean mirroring a reddish-orange sky produced by a California wildfire.

"What's your name?" I asked.

His eyes rose above the flames to stare into mine. "I believe people around here have decided to call me 'Ghost,' right?"

"You know about that?" Of course, he knew about that. I don't know why I asked such a stupid question...

He didn't respond. He just stared at me for a moment longer and stood up. It startled me. As he pushed himself off of the ground, I flinched. He retrieved a bucket of water and doused the flames. The fire was reduced to a fast-moving upward surge of steam and smoke that reeked of sulfur, and the cold, soot-filled water flowed from the base of the smoldering pile of wooden statues and soaked my pants. "Dude, what the hell?" I said as I sprung to my feet. I looked down and noticed that not only were my pants and shoes wet, but

the ash had also blackened them. A puddle began to sur-
round me.

'The Ghost' tossed a tattered backpack on a small
metal table that was reddened by a layer of rust. He dug his
hand inside and felt around for something, and I anticipated
he was searching for a weapon.

"Listen, I'll leave. I'm sorry," I said with a quivering
voice.

He stared at me with confusion as he pulled out a
sandwich bag filled with joints and a severely dented silver
Zippo lighter.

"It's just weed, kid."

"Why did you pour water on me?" I asked with an au-
dible mix of fear and anger in my voice.

"Because you need water to put out a fire."

"You could've said something."

"We could do a lot of things, but we don't." He said as
he placed the joint between his dry lips. He attempted to
light it, but the Zippo didn't produce a flame, just sparks. He
pounded the lighter on the table. I flinched.

"Stop with the theatrics. I'm not gonna do anything
to ya, you little shit. It's just low on fluid. You gotta better
chance of it working if you bang it around a bit, see?"

He flicked the lighter again, and like he said it would,
it worked. The scent of marijuana filled the air and

overpowered the damp, sulfuric fumes that lingered from the charred statues. He sat down on a metal chair with faded black letters across the backrest that read: PROPERTY OF U.S. NAVY 1977. There were labels like that on nearly everything the Navy left behind in the warehouse. Something as small as a metal cup or as ordinary as a table was branded as a United States military product. Any system that is powerful enough to upend democratically-elected governments and petty enough to add a stamp of bureaucracy to the production of a single cup is a system you should be afraid of.

"So, kid, what do you want?"

"I'm a student journalist and... I want to do a report about you for my final."

He stared at me for a moment, and then his eyes moved downward. There was shame in his eyes. He took a slow drag off of his joint and slowly exhaled.

"That's actually very kind of you to consider me, but there's nothing to report, and I'm not newsworthy."

"But you are," I said. "Everyone in town wonders about you, and there's even like... local myths about why you make your statues. You're kind of a famous enigma."

"A famous enigma, huh? An enigma is someone who's a mystery, right?" He asked sarcastically. "I'm not an enigma; you guys just make shit up about me. A mystery is something difficult to solve. Anyone could ask me, and I'd tell 'em why I create; I do it, so hopefully, one day, I can be... *forgiven.*"

"So, you'll let me do the interview?"

He deeply inhaled and began to laugh. The laugh turned into a coughing spell, flinging smoke and mucus out of his mouth. The fit instantly turned his brilliant blue eyes red. He hawked a loogie and wiped all the excess moisture from his face with the sleeve of his jacket. His jacket was filthy, and he didn't care. Our eyes met, and he said, "Pull up a chair, kid." I dragged a rusted chair, covered in thick cobwebs, to the table he was sitting at and pulled out my cell phone.

"It is okay to record the conversation?"

"What's your name, kid?"

"Benjamin, but I go by Ben."

"Well, that's a logical thing to go by, Ben. If your name's Benjamin and you decided you wanted to be called Ralph, I'd wonder what the fuck was wrong with you. Not even people named Ralph want to be called Ralph."

"What's your name?" I asked as I wiped old spider webs from the chair and sat down.

"Ralph."

"Really?"

"Yes, no one named Ralph lies about the misfortune of being named Ralph. The female equivalent is Karen, my mother's name."

I chuckled. 'The Ghost' or Ralph had a sense of humor. I was still nervous, but seeing him go from tearful and cryptic to sarcastic and self-deprecating made me more confident that the interview would go well.

"So, I can record, right?"

"Go ahead," He said with a smirk as he lit another joint.

"What's your full name?"

"Ralph Alexander Wilcotts Jr."

"Where are you from? Are you from Vallejo or somewhere else in The Bay Area?"

"I wish I was from The Bay Area, but I'm from Michigan."

"Where in Michigan?"

"Warren. It's a town just outside of Detroit."

"So, how did you get here?"

"How much do you want to know?"

"I want to know everything."

"Okay..."

"When I was a kid, I always enjoyed creating. First, it started with drawing. I used to draw superheroes and people I loved, and I'd tape them to the walls of my house. Not just my room, but all over the house. My father would come home from work and tear the drawings down. He would throw them in the trash, but I kept drawing. This happened every day. I'd go to school, and right when I got home, I'd sit in my room, and I'd draw for hours. Michigan is really cold in the winter and miserably humid in the summer, so being outside wasn't great like it is here in California. If I was living in a warehouse in Michigan, I would have froze to death a long time ago."

"Your dad wasn't supportive of your drawing?"

"He wasn't supportive of anything or anyone. He wasn't a builder, and he called himself one, but he wasn't. He destroyed everything he touched."

"What do you mean he 'called himself a builder?'"

"He worked at the Ford automotive factory in Detroit. He worked on the assembly line there until I was 12; the day he was laid off from Ford was the day things got bad. Really bad."

"How so?"

Ralph paused for a moment, his eyes glossed over, and he stared into the distance. He crushed the cherry of the joint with the tip of his fingers. Then, without a moment of hesitation, he reached into his sandwich bag and lit another. He took a deep drag and exhaled the smoke with a sigh and said, "Before he would just come home and throw away my drawings. He would verbally attack me, but he rarely hit me. He was too tired from the factory to hit me, but once he got laid off, it seemed that was all he had the energy to do. He beat the artist out of me. By the time I was 13, I didn't draw anymore."

"I'm really sorry, Ralph."

He looked at me, the blueness of his eyes barely visible as the marijuana turned them into little more than slits. He took another hit and passed me the joint. I don't know why, but I took it from him. I placed it in my mouth and breathed in deeply, and coughed harder than I thought was humanly possible.

"Got them virgin lungs, huh, Ben?"

"I don't usually smoke weed; this is maybe the 5th or 6th time I've done it," I replied between coughs

"I didn't smoke weed in high school either. The first time I smoked, I probably coughed even harder than you did."

"I'm not a huge party person, and it distracts me from my homework. I am pretty driven to go far in school so I can be a journalist. A real one. I'd love to write for the Chronicle, and I think about it a lot. I know it's San Francisco, and there's a ton of people there who are always high, but I want my stories to be smart and fun. If you want to write a great story, you have to keep yourself sharp."

"Yeah, but sometimes life is about more than documenting it; you gotta live it sometimes, too."

In a way, I knew that he was right, but I didn't feel like justifying the method I had perceived as the best way to reach my goals to him or anyone else, so I continued with the interview.

"What did you do after you stopped drawing?"

"I'd stay out instead of coming home. I'd hang out at the lake, or I'd go to Downtown Detroit with my friends. I made a best friend. Tim. His name was Tim... Tim was... Tim."

Ralph's eyes shifted suddenly every time he said "Tim." It was bizarre. Everything about Ralph was strange on a surface level, but the way his eyes jolted and widened when reminiscing about Tim truly startled me. There was a madness that could be seen inside of him.

"Tell me about Tim."

"He taught me a lot about myself, and it led to a lot of shit in my life."

"How'd you and Tim become friends?"

"He betrayed me!" Ralph screamed as he slammed his fist into his mouth. He continued to punch himself in the face and grunt. I just sat there. Frozen. My fear had returned. Blood and saliva dribbled out of his mouth. Ralph suddenly became the 'The Ghost' to me again. His humanity was stripped away by my nerves... Again.

"How did he betray you?"

Ralph's eyes were pointed directly at me, but he didn't see me. He was looking past me — through me. The blood that coated his beard was crimson, and it didn't look like normal bleeding. The backdrop provided by the whiteness of his facial hair gave it a warm glow. His blood had visual qualities that one may first interpret as supernatural, but upon further inspection, he would realize that no exceptional or unexplained influence existed here. The only abnormality was mental. The weight of the psychological burden that forced his fists to mangle his flesh was far more difficult to comprehend than the hue of the liquid that spilled from the blunt force.

"He lived a lie and killed me with my truth."

"What does that mean?"

"Tim was the only friend that would come with me to the abandoned parts of Detroit. Everyone went Downtown, but that was it. They were scared. There were abandoned houses and big industrial buildings, kinda like this all over Detroit. Tim would go; everybody else was too pussy. They were scared some black folks were gonna rob 'em."

"So, basically, how people around here treat Oakland?"

"No. Oakland has life; Detroit is death with a zip code."

"Hmm... That was strangely... Poetic. So what happened in Detroit?"

"At first, nothing. We'd break into boarded-up homes, buildings, and other abandoned places and find stuff. Sometimes really cool stuff: movies, toys, books, and other times we'd find crazy shit. I can't tell you how many times we would sneak into some weirdo place and find bums or drug dealers, and then we'd run like hell. It hurts to know that I'm what I would have run from when I was a kid, but in truth, there's no such thing as youthful nostalgia without longing and lingering but distant pain. I don't believe I'm alone in that feeling. I think it's the same way for everyone. It's just more openly visible with someone like me."

"What do you mean by someone like you?"

"I mean the homeless wear their pain. The scars manifest in actual filth. There's no junk drawer to put the garbage you're emotionally attached to in. No quiet room to sit and cry in. It's all done outside. It's public. Everyone knows something is wrong, but no one says a word about it. They just hide behind their walls that hold up their roofs, and they go insane. Quietly. People aren't afraid of me because they don't understand. They're afraid that they do."

"So, how did Tim betray you? I'm not trying to force you to talk. You can end this interview at any time; I just think it's significant. It seems that way, at least."

Ralph looked at me with a sudden focus and asked, "your name's Ben, right?"

"Yes," I replied.

"You a faggot, Ben?"

"What?"

"It's okay. I am. Do you understand?"

"I'm not gay if that's what you mean? And what does that ha...."

"It has a lot to do with a lot," he interjected.

"Is that related to Tim?"

"Tim and I would explore the ruins of Detroit. We were alone together a lot. One day we were drinking in an abandoned house on Detroit's East Side. We were bonding over us both having shitty fathers who sat at home all day waiting on a phone call from a car company that would never come. Before it got boarded up, whoever lived in the house we were at left a stereo system with a tape deck and record player attached. The place still had electricity. Which was pretty fuckin' weird lookin' back on it. Tim had a David Bowie cassette, and we put it in the tape deck, and the thing worked. We sat there, drunk as shit listening to "The Man

Who Sold The World," and he kissed me. I kissed him back...
And my life as I knew it began to end."

Ralph's eyes shifted toward the floor. "My father
didn't have much use for me before, but learning that his son
was a fag gave him all the excuse he needed to get rid of
me."

"How did he even find out?" I asked.

The shame in Ralph's eyes had been replaced with
what I could only describe as a latent rage: a hatred never
genuinely expressed in full form. It is the type of rage that
isn't a result of global injustice but the pain of letting some-
one inside your sanctuary, only for them to burn it down.

"I don't like to talk about this, but I will because no
one talks to me at all, and it's nice to hear a voice that isn't
an echo of my own now and then."

And then there was silence... It didn't last for more
than 30 or 40 seconds, but it felt longer. I was uncomforta-
ble, and I wanted the silence to end. "Are you still capable of
hope?" I asked.

He focused his glare on me.

"Anyone is capable of anything. It's something you
learn, Ben. And once you learn, you shouldn't forget it."

And I wouldn't...

"Tim and I spent time together whenever we could,
which was pretty much all the time. We didn't explore

Detroit's ruins as much and went to the same house on Detroit's East Side. It was basically our second home, and nobody came to bother us; they were all too scared. We had it all there. We had electricity, music, and most importantly, we had each other. At least I believed that we did."

His blue eyes blazed with brightness as he reminisced about the moments he shared in the abandoned house on Detroit's East Side with Tim.

"We listened to music! We listened to so much music. We used to go to the record stores and find good deals on tapes, and we'd save our lunch money and buy them to bring back to the house. We'd listen to all the good shit: David Bowie, ACDC, Queen, Velvet Underground, Michael Jackson, Prince. We used to argue over who was better, Michael or Prince. We both knew it was Michael, he wouldn't admit it, but I knew that he knew. That's not to take anything away from Prince; he was such a talented artist!"

"It sounds like Tim meant a lot to you."

"Everything was too good to be true, so naturally, it wasn't."

Discomfort. I felt discomfort but a subtle fascination. I never truly understood how a single event could shape or disfigure someone in such a permanent way. However, I was about to find out. One event can change everything. Humans are fragile. Ralph was human; Ralph was fragile. He wasn't a ghost. Even if everyone around him pretended he was, he wasn't.

"We were on the porch of the abandoned house. Our house. On the entire street, there were only two homes that had people living in them. The neighborhood was shit, but the street was quiet, it had already been destroyed, there was nothing left to take, or so I thought."

"Did you guys get beat up or robbed?" I genuinely asked.

He smiled. "That would have honestly been preferable," he said. "I would have gladly gotten the shit kicked out of me by every thug in Detroit rather than what actually happened."

"So, what did happen?"

"Cops. Or a cop. The dad of one of our friends was a Detroit city cop. Even though barely anyone lived on the street where we hung out, the cops used to patrol the shit out of East Detroit. It was black and poor, and several blocks of it were abandoned. It was an ideal place for cops to kick the living shit out of people without any repercussions."

"Were you arrested?"

ALSO AVAILABLE FROM

TERRAN EMPIRE PUBLISHING

The Fallen **Series by Alex Stargazer**

The Fallen series takes the reader to a far-future Ireland where an oppressive political regime holds the people in check with a draconian social hierarchy program designed to keep the masses docile and in their place. When Upperclassmen Conall comes across a Fallen boy named Mark, a split-second decision would forever change his buttoned-up life as a politician's son. Thrown into the political intrigue of the time, Conall must navigate the perils of inter-class mingling and his growing sense of love and desire for Mark while trying to stay one step ahead of the Party and the supernatural forces at play. Add in spell casting witches, flying cars, Communist rebels, and the literal Devil, and you have the makings of a romantic tale that will keep readers glued to every page!

Made in the USA
Las Vegas, NV
15 March 2022